MAXIMUN IMPACT

I0143202

2018

By Dr. Delron Shirley

Cover design by Jeremy Shirley
Maps Courtesy of Andrew Foundation

Table of Contents

Introduction

A number of years ago, I ran across an article that is now probably safely filed away in an extinct cabinet at the university where I no longer teach. Although I can't get my hands on the original document today, I distinctly remember that it listed the conversion of Saul of Tarsus on the road to Damascus as one of the one hundred most pivotal events in all of human history. In fact, I seem to remember that it was very close to the top and that the life of Jesus wasn't even included at all. Why would a secular historian make such an evaluation? I think it is because that even though Jesus brought salvation to the human race, it was this radical evangelist/theologian who took that experience and made maximum impact with it. Just think of all the sermons you have heard and try to calculate what percentage of them were based on Paul's writing versus the sayings of Jesus. I remember one pastor who gave a series of messages on the epistles of Peter; however, there was not one session in which he didn't mistakenly say, "Paul" when he intended to say "Peter" because he was so accustomed to preaching from Paul's epistles.

According to his own testimony, Saul (by this time known as Paul) fully preached the gospel from Jerusalem all the way to Illyricum in northwest Greece (Romans 15:19) and intended to carry the message as far as Spain – considered at that time to be the end of the earth (Romans 15:24). According to his testimony in Romans 15:21-23, Paul had totally evangelized eastern Europe and western Asia. His reports in Colossians 1:23, Romans 1:8, Romans 15:20, 15:23, and I Thessalonians 1:8 conclude that his gospel message had penetrated the whole world during his lifetime. Remember, this was before mass communication – no radio, television, internet … not even printed books!

Plus, this was before any form of speedy transportation – no planes, trains, or automobiles. This determined evangelist had to travel on foot or, if lucky, on horseback. Even when he sailed on ships, the journeys were slow – dependent upon winds and ocean currents and necessitating months-long layovers during seasons of inclement weather.

Church tradition reports that the original twelve apostles of Jesus spread throughout the then-known world – with Andrew becoming a missionary to southern Russia around the Black Sea after ministering in Greece and Asia Minor, Simon Peter doing evangelistic and missionary work among the Jews going as far as Babylon (a code name for Rome), John the Beloved serving as the bishop in Ephesus before being exiled to the penal island of Patmos off Turkey, James the son of Zebedee ministering in Jerusalem and Judea, Philip going to Hieropolis of Phrygia, Matthew being martyred in Ethiopia, Bartholomew serving in Armenia, Thomas laboring in Parthia, Persia, and India and eventually suffering martyrdom in southern India, James the son of Alphaeus preaching in Palestine and Egypt, Jude preaching in Assyria and Persia and dying as a martyr in Persia, Simon the Zealot preaching in Israel, and Nathanael continuing the ministry near Nazareth. However, if we study the history of Christianity in these regions, we generally find that they date their heritage to much later events that are associated with Christians who trace their lineage back to the ministry of the Apostle Paul. Russia, for instance, views the baptism of Prince Vladimir by a Byzantine priest in the eleventh century as their Christian genesis. Although Christianity flourished in the Middle East and North Africa during the early centuries of the Christian era, it was basically eradicated with the rise of Islam. The re-introduction of the faith came through the efforts of ministers and laymen from the Western churches that hearken back to Paul's influence. The story in India is a bit different in that when the famous

Portuguese explorer Vasco da Gama opened the first Europe-India sea route in 1498, he was surprised to find Christians who traced their heritage to converts who were baptized by Thomas in AD 52. Two years later, eight Franciscan priests, eight chaplains, and a chaplain major arrived and introduced the Catholic faith – the Pauline influence. By 1504, it was reported that there were thirty thousand Christian families in some twenty towns and a great number of villages. Although there is no clarification as to how much of that Christian community predated the advent of the Pauline influence, it is clear that the community numbers skyrocketed once the Catholic persuasion entered, swelling the Christian population to more than two hundred thousand within the next seventy-five years compared to the persistent but limited growth of the faith over the previous fourteen and a half centuries.

So who was this man who made such an impact upon the world and infused the church with such powerful DNA? Let's explore this question through several different avenues: the story of his life, examples of the people he impacted, and his own personal confession of what made him the man he was.

Paul's Life Story

Our first introduction to Paul is as Saul of Tarsus, a persecutor of the early Christians. However, it is possible for us to piece together a bit of the history that led up to this chapter in his life. Saul grew up as a freeborn Roman citizen (Acts 22:28) in the city of Tarsus, which he called "no mean city," indicating that it was far above the average city of his time. (Acts 21:39) It was certainly no average place in that it was a major center of commerce, education, and military power. With the excellent education that his writings demonstrate that Paul possessed and his Roman privilege coupled with the strong ethic his Jewish upbringing afforded him, Paul would have been a success in any field he would have chosen to pursue: business, military, academics, etc. Yet, he chose to abandon any of these lucrative pursuits and give himself to the study of theology at the rabbinic school of Gamaliel in Jerusalem (Acts 22:3), a career that rendered him so little financial security that he had to augment his livelihood by making tents. (Acts 18:3) The biblical records indicate that Saul was bothered by anything that deviated from the theological doctrines he had learned in the synagogue and the rabbinical school; that's why he was persecuting the church. (Acts 9:2) He was adamant that the Christian movement – which he considered to be a blasphemous perversion of the Jewish faith – be crushed to death before it had a chance to spread its infectious heresy any further. As a personal disciple of Gamaliel – who is recognized even until today as one of the ten greatest rabbis in Jewish history – Saul gained an excellent command of biblical and traditional knowledge and the expertise to expound on these concepts, and it is also likely that he gained influence in the Jewish community through his association with the prominent rabbi and Sanhedrin member. (Acts 5:34)

It was probably this association that afforded him access to the high priest who granted him papers to go to Damascus in his attempt to eliminate the Christian faith before it penetrated this pivotal city. (Acts 9:2) In this request, we gain a great insight into strategic thinking of our subject. Damascus was a terminal and transit point for all the major trade routes of the time – the frankincense route coming out of the Arabian Peninsula, the gold route coming out of Africa, and the silk route coming out of the Far East – all connecting to the Roman highway system that brought these goods to the capital of the world. Saul knew that if this new religion were able to become entrenched in the city of Damascus it would soon spread like a contagious disease along these corridors of commerce until it had infected the entire known world. Thus, he used his influence, connections, and eloquence to gain permission to implement his strategic plan to excise this religious "cancer" before it entered the bloodstream of the society.

Conversion and Early Ministry

Of course, it was on this campaign that he encountered Jesus and was converted to the faith that he was so adamantly persecuting and attempting to eradicate. Acts chapter nine describes the dramatic encounter that has become known as the Damascus Road Experience in which Saul was knocked to the ground and blinded by the brilliant light that emanated from the Risen Christ. Those with him were also impacted by the encounter but did not hear the words that Jesus spoke to His captive that day, "Saul, Saul, why persecutest thou me? I am Jesus whom thou persecutest: it is hard for thee to kick against the pricks. Arise, and go into the city, and it shall be told thee what thou must do." (Acts 9:4-6) With the help of his companions, the blinded crusader found his way to a home on the main street of the city of Damascus – Straight Street, so named because it was the major thoroughfare running straight through the middle of the city. After three days of fasting and soul searching, Saul's conversion was completed when the Lord sent a reluctant evangelist to find him. When the Lord spoke to Ananias, he immediately refused with the logical objection that Saul's only motive for being in Damascus was to arrest Christians – and Ananias could think of a whole lot of better things to do that day than to walk directly into such a trap. The Lord continued to deal with His messenger, telling him that He had already shown Paul a vision of a man by the specific name of Ananias coming to him. With that kind of preannouncement before the Lord even spoke to him about the assignment, Ananias decided that there really wasn't an alternative. As he agreed to go, the Lord gave Ananias further instructions to bring to the humbled man on Straight Street, "Go thy way: for he is a chosen vessel unto me, to bear my name before the Gentiles, and kings, and the children of Israel: For I will shew him how great things he must suffer for my name's sake." (Acts 9:15-16) Through Ananias' ministry that day, Saul was healed, baptized in water, and filled with the Holy Spirit.

The historical record of Acts doesn't include the next step in the chronological sequence of our new convert's life, but we know from Paul's own writings that it took some time for him to process all that had happened to him. Although it seems from the story in Acts 9:20 that Paul began his proclamations right away, Galatians 1:17 makes it clear that this time of introspection came before he began to preach in Damascus. In Galatians 1:11-12, Paul described his understanding of theology and doctrine as a gift directly from Jesus, not an academic achievement from his books and mentors, "But I certify you, brethren, that the gospel which was preached of me is not after man. For I neither received it of man, neither was I taught it, but by the revelation of Jesus Christ." We can easily see how Saul – who excelled in his knowledge of and belief in the Old Testament truths as they had been conveyed to him through his Jewish heritage, religious traditions, and rabbinic interpretations (Philippians 3:4-6, Acts 22:3, Galatians 1:13-14) – would be totally disoriented and confused when he suddenly encountered the Risen Jesus and discovered that He was indeed the true messiah, not a blasphemous imposter as Saul had supposed from the years he had spent poring over the writings of his Jewish faith. In that dramatic encounter in the dust of the road to Damascus, Paul's spirit cried out an acknowledgement that his head refused to accept. Before his head could reason out the situation, his heart erupted out of his mouth, acclaiming Jesus as Lord. (Acts 9:5-6) Immediately, he found himself in a quandary, trying to reconcile the contradiction between the interpretation he held of Old Testament truths (which he could not abandon because he was still convinced that they were the Word of God) and the supernatural revelation he had just received. The result was, as he described it in Galatians, a gift – a revelation, an impartation, a supernatural insight. It was so powerfully personal to him that he felt confident to refer to it with such personally possessive phrases as "my gospel" (Romans 2:16, 16:25, II Timothy 2:8) and "our gospel" (II Corinthians 4:3, I Thessalonians 1:5, II Thessalonians 2:14). In order to process these conflicting revelations until they became this gospel that was so personally his own, Saul headed into the desert of Arabia and remained there for three years. (Galatians 1:17-18) Although there is no record of exactly what happened during this period of isolation, he most certainly spent that time comparing his Old Testament knowledge with the revelation he had just received from Jesus. There must have been long days of study and lengthy seasons of prayer – struggling with every scripture and each tradition – until he was able to attest without any sense of contradiction that the Old Testament is indeed holy, just, and good and that it is a schoolmaster bringing us to the revelation of Christ. (Romans 7:12, Galatians 3:24)

Armed with this clear revelation of the gospel, Saul returned to Damascus and went out to preach – a campaign that made him the target of a death plot by the Jewish leaders in the city. When the scheme became known, the Christians in the city slipped him away to safety by dropping him over the city wall in a basket at night after the gates had been locked and the city had "rolled up the sidewalks" for the night. Escaping to Jerusalem, Saul desired to associate with the believers there but did not find them welcoming since they, like Ananias, feared that his conversion was only a ploy to get inside information that would lead to raids, arrests, trials, and executions. Fortunately, one person believed him and helped him gain acceptance – Barnabas. Before long, Saul created quite a stir in the city by preaching the gospel that he had so vehemently opposed, again resulting in death threats and the need for him to be smuggled out of town. This exit was apparently initiated by a visionary encounter that Paul mentioned during his address to the mob at the temple at the time of his arrest. (Acts 22:17-21) He escaped to Caesarea (the Roman administrative headquarters on the Mediterranean coast) and then to his hometown of Tarsus.

The Jerusalem Council and the First Missionary Journey

Meanwhile, something new was happening in the church. Peter was called to preach to a gentile audience, and – contrary to what everyone would have anticipated – the Holy Spirit fell on them! In another unexpected turn of events, Greeks in the Syrian city of Antioch were accepting the gospel. Surveying this unprecedented move of God, Barnabas knew that there was only one man with a clear enough revelation of the universal nature of the gospel to become God's spokesman to these unconventional converts – Saul. Therefore, he went to Tarsus and convinced Saul to come to Antioch (one of the most important cities in the eastern Mediterranean region – actually rivalling Alexandria, Egypt, as the chief city of the Near East area – because of its geographical, military, and economic position and the fact that it dominated the spice trade, the silk routes, and the Persian Royal Road) where he would live and minister for the following year (Acts 11:26) until the two of them were commissioned to travel to Jerusalem with an offering to help the believers who were suffering due to a famine (Acts 11:27-30). Upon their return to Antioch, the Lord directed the leadership that Barnabas and Saul had further traveling assignments; so, after fasting and prayer, they laid hands on them and sent them out as the church's first official missionaries. (Acts 13:4) Even though the Holy Spirit's explicit direction was that Barnabas and Saul be ordained to this work, they also took John Mark (Acts 13:5) although he was not specifically called for the task – a decision that eventually proved to be an issue (Acts 15:36-39). This first journey took these new missionaries through Seleucia (the capital city of previous empires in the region), Cyprus (an island that was of such strategic significance that it was constantly under conquest by the major Mediterranean powers), Salamis (an island with significance as a port for naval and merchant ships), Paphos (the capital city of the region), Perga in Pamphylia (the capital city of the area; from here John Mark parted company and returned to Jerusalem), Antioch in Pisidia (considered to be the crossroads of the Mediterranean, Aegean and Central Anatolian regions), Iconium (capital of Lycaonia), Lystra (a Roman colonial city from which they governed the tribes in the mountains to the west), and Derbe (a city of enough consequence to mint its own coinage). On their return, Barnabas and Saul retraced their steps through Lystra, Iconium, Antioch in Pisidia, Pamphylia, Perga, and

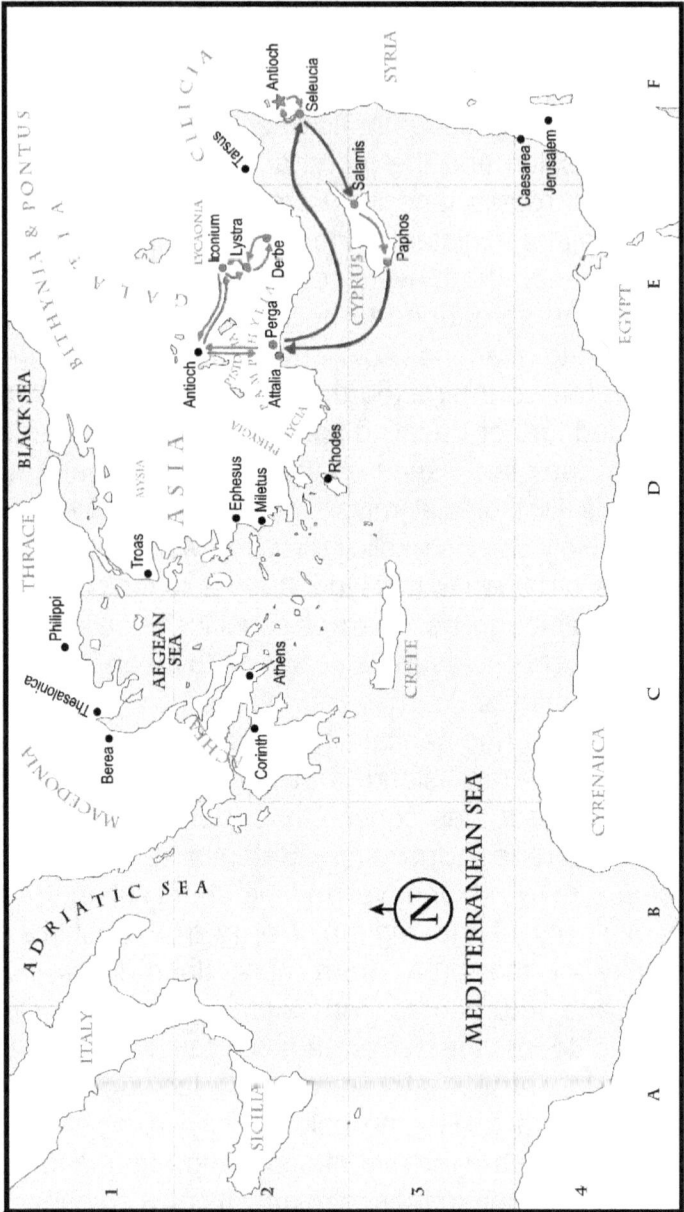

Paul's First Mission Journey

Attalia (modern-day Antalya, Turkey's biggest international sea resort) before sailing back to Antioch. (Acts chapters 13 and 14) This lengthy journey was marked by several characteristic qualities of Paul's ministry methodology. In Paphos, he confronted a sorcerer who was controlled by a demonic spirit that hindered Paul from ministering to Sergius Paulus who was open to the gospel message. After binding the spirit, Paul was able to help the official believe. (Acts 13:6-12) This episode illustrates two of the basic principles of Paul's impactful ministry. First, it demonstrated the exercise of spiritual weapons that confront the forces of evil head-on and free the minds of men to hear and understand the gospel. (II Corinthians 10:3-5) Second, it represented his approach that the gospel should be ministered to people in positions of authority as a way to bring its influence into a community from the top down – producing maximum impact. (I Timothy 2:1-2) In fact, this approach was revealed to him from the very day of his initial encounter with Jesus. (Acts 9:15) In Pisidia (Acts 13:14) and Iconium (Acts 14:1), he preached first to the Jews and then to the gentiles when the Jews refused his message – in direct accordance to his proposed evangelistic approach (Romans 1:16). In Lystra, he ministered healing to a man who had been disabled from birth as proof of the validity of his message (Acts 14:8-10) – a strategy that he advocated as the primary approach for introducing the gospel (Romans 15:18-20). As a result of this miraculous healing, the local people wanted to acclaim him a deity, but Paul refused the accolades – an action that opened the door for his opponents to turn the people against him to the extent that they stoned him and left him for dead. It was likely this near-death or out-of-the-body experience that he described in II Corinthians 12:2-4. Again, one of Paul's life principles surfaces here – the willingness to give his life for the gospel that he preached. (Romans 9:3, II

Corinthians 12:15)

When a division occurred in the church over the practice of circumcision, Paul and Barnabas became delegates to the council in Jerusalem that was called to establish an official church policy on the issue. (Acts chapter 15) According to a parallel account in Galatians 2:1-9, Paul took Titus with him as a test case to prove the point that a gentile believer could be a genuine convert without having to submit to the Jewish ritual. When the final verdict was handed down, the ruling was in Paul's favor – circumcision was not obligatory. However, when we turn the page to chapter sixteen, we find the story of Paul's selection of Timothy as an understudy. Amazingly, the first thing that Paul did – immediately after his victory in the council of elders and apostles in Jerusalem – was to circumcise Timothy. Why? Because Timothy was destined for leadership in the church. Had he been just a layman, Timothy would have fallen under the auspices of Paul's teaching in Galatians 5:6, "For in Jesus Christ neither circumcision availeth any thing, nor uncircumcision; but faith which worketh by love," and Paul would not have required him to submit to the ritual. On the other hand, Paul knew that this young man needed to live by a higher standard so that his message would never be challenged. Paul himself gave up many privileges that he knew were permissible for him under grace in order to maintain an untarnished standard before those with whom he wanted to share the gospel. (I Corinthians 6:12, 8:6-13, 10:23) Along with the ruling that circumcision was not necessary, the council did set up some other standards that they felt were necessary in order for the new gentile converts to not be offensive to their more traditional Jewish brethren, "That ye abstain from meats offered to idols, and from blood, and from things strangled, and from fornication." (Acts 15:29) Interestingly, Paul agreed to these conditions but enforced them according to his own terms. In Acts 21:25 he failed to mention the issue of meat sacrificed to idols all together, and in his writings he said that it was a matter of conscience (I Corinthians 8:4-13).

Second Missionary Journey

Accompanied by Silas – a leader from the Jerusalem church who had returned to Antioch with Paul and Barnabas in order to verify the decision of the council – Paul's second journey took him through the regions of Syria and Cilicia (Acts 15:41) to the cities of Derbe and Lystra (Acts 16:1) and onward to the regions of Phrygia (the home of the fabled King Midas who turned everything he touched into gold) and the region of Galatia (a client-state of the Roman empire which served as an administrative center) as far as Mysia where the Holy Spirit directed them that they should not go into Asia Minor (Acts 16:6). When they came to the seaport city of Troas (this chief port of northwest Asia Minor with a population of close to one hundred thousand prospered greatly in Roman times and became a free and autonomous city), Paul had a vision of a Macedonian man calling for him to come there to help. His immediate response was to board a ship to Neapolis (the major harbor of this region) and onward to Philippi (a city that was significant because of the local gold mines and important trade routes that passed through it) – the first landfall of the gospel on European shores. (Acts 16:9-12) His stay in Philippi was again marked by many of the characteristics of his ministry methodology: he went first to a place where prayers were customarily made (apparently, there was no official synagogue in the city), he then confronted the demonic spirit that held the hearts, minds, and lives of the people in bondage, and finally he put his own life on the line for the gospel when he was arrested and beaten. (Acts 16:13-24) In these stories, we see two more aspects of his ministry methodology. The principle of discipleship was exemplified in the lives of two individuals that Paul met in this city. When Lydia responded to his message by the river side, Paul went to her home and mentored her in the faith (Acts 16:15); he did the same thing for the jailer and his family after they believed (Acts 16:34). In his epistles to the young man Timothy whom he circumcised during this period of time, Paul expressed the significance of this sort of personal discipleship by reminding this protégé of how he had mentored him and challenged him to continue the practice with others who would in turn perpetuate it into future generations. (II Timothy 2:2) The story of Paul and Silas' miraculous deliverance from the prison showcases another of Paul's mission strategies – praise. In his letter to the Romans, Paul made an archetypal statement when he talked about dealing with troubles, "glory in tribulations also: knowing that tribulation worketh patience; And patience, experience; and experience, hope." (Romans 5:2-4) From these verses, it is easy to see that this great apostle of the faith didn't count temptation and troubles as occasions for discouragement. Rather, temptation was an occasion for praising the Lord. Joy and rejoicing were his response when the devil tried to get him down. He knew that he needed strength, and it is likely that he remembered that Nehemiah had said, "The joy of the Lord is your strength." (Nehemiah 8:10) When he and Silas were in that prison in Philippi, they proved that joy rather than discouragement was the best response to trouble. They had been beaten, imprisoned, and held in chains; yet, at midnight – when everything was the darkest – they were singing and praising God. Through their praises, an earthquake delivered them from the jail. Not only did their praise physically open the door to the jail, it also opened the door of opportunity for Paul to win the jailer and his family to Christ – a great ministry strategy.

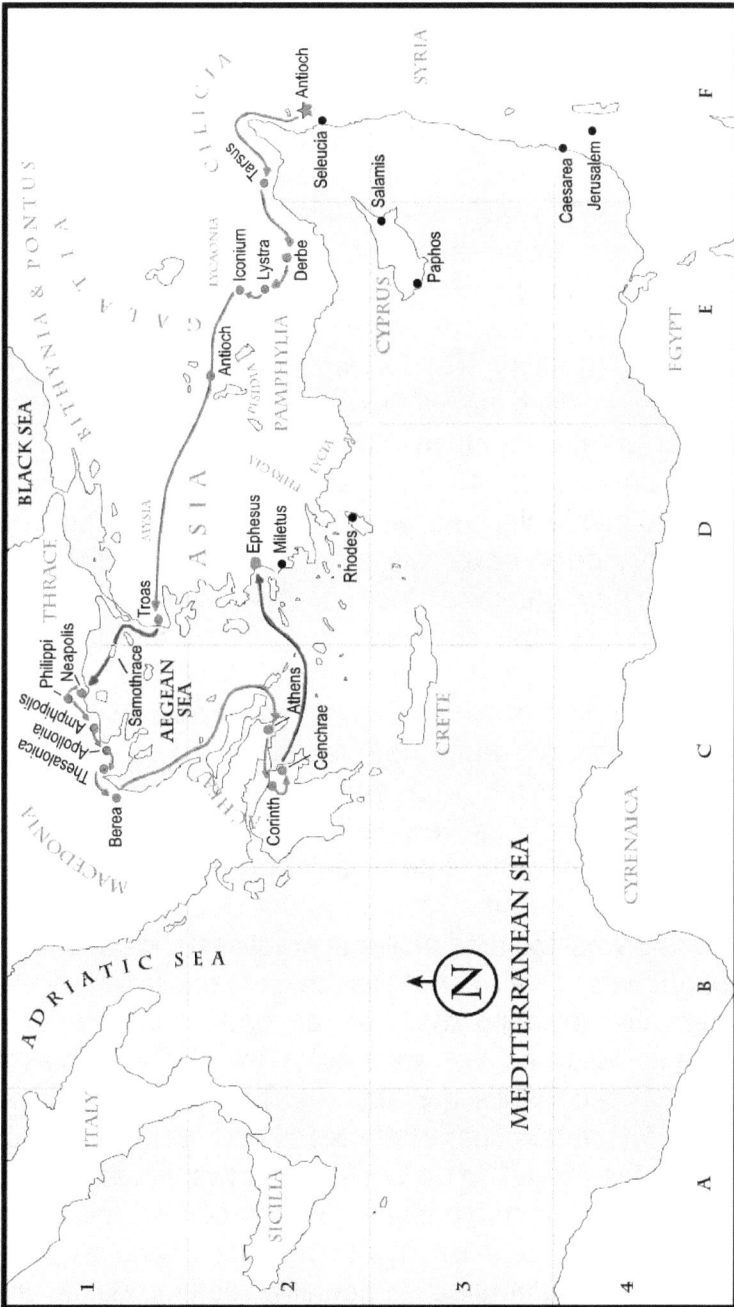

Paul's Second Mission Journey

From Philippi, Paul and Silas passed through Amphipolis (a city of military significance dating back as far as the time of Alexander the Great) and Appolonia (home to a renowned school of philosophy) and came to Thessalonica (known as the "co-capital" since it was the region's second major economic, industrial, commercial, and political center and a major transportation hub with a thriving commercial port) where Paul taught for just three short weeks – again following his typical ministry pattern of approaching the Jews first. (Acts 17:1-9) It was in Thessalonica that Paul and Silas received the accusation that should be understood as their greatest acclaim – that they had turned the world upside down! (Acts 17:6) Talk about maximum impact!! It was also in this city – as we will see later in our study – that Paul did indeed have maximum impact even though the narrative here compares the reception that Paul received in Berea (a city that controlled the water sources for the territory) – the next stop on his evangelistic tour – by saying that the people of Berea "were more noble than those in Thessalonica, in that they received the word with all readiness of mind, and searched the scriptures daily, whether those things were so." (Acts 17:11) But before we leave the story of the three-week stay in Thessalonica, we should note one other aspect about Paul's ministry there. When he was accused of illegal practices and his case was brought before the rulers of the city, the officials let him go – essentially declaring that he had broken no laws. This incident illustrates yet another of the life principles that characterized Paul's ministry – obedience to the laws of man. In Romans chapter thirteen, Paul went into detail to express the obligation for Christians to respect and obey the legal powers. In this passage, Paul made it explicitly clear that Christians are to live in total respect for and submission to the civil authorities – actually recognizing them as ministers of God – a concept that we will discuss in detail later.

After teaching some in Berea, Paul departed ahead of Silas and Timothy, southward into the Achaia region of southern Greece to Athens (one of the oldest and most significant cities in world history). (Acts 17:14-15) While there, Paul was moved by the prevalent idolatry of the city and decided to preach to the intellectuals who gathered on Mars Hill for philosophical discussion and debate. The end result of his elaborate message that is recorded in great detail in Acts chapter seventeen was that a few men and one woman believed. It is quite noticeable that this sermon is distinctly different from all the other sermons of Paul that are recorded in the book of Acts and the messages that are preserved in his epistles – an idea that will be explored further in another section. However, before we leave the discussion of the ministry in Athens, it would be good to mention that Paul was so concerned for the new believers in Thessalonica that he sent Timothy back to check up on them. (I Thessalonians 3:1-7) This act demonstrated another principle that characterized Paul's ministry ethic – care for the churches. In fact, he actually described that the emotional weight he carried for these new believers was even more taxing than the physical obstacles he endures – including his beatings and his imprisonments. (II Corinthians 11:23-28)

From Athens, Paul traveled the fifty-two miles to Corinth (a major seaport in that it was located on a narrow isthmus that allowed merchants to transport their goods overland for a short distance and avoid lengthy and expensive journeys at sea) where he stayed a year and a half. (Acts 18:1, 18:5, 18:11) There, Paul met Aquila and Priscilla who had come from Rome when Claudius Caesar banished all the Jews over an issue concerning "Chrestus," which we assume to be a misspelling of "Christus," meaning Christ. After Silas and Timothy rejoined Paul in Corinth, he wrote his first letter to the Thessalonian believers. (I Thessalonians 3:1-2, 3:6) Shortly afterward, he followed up with his second epistle to them. Paul's ministry in Corinth followed his usual pattern of ministering first to the Jewish community before turning to the gentile population. (Acts 18:5-6) As so often happened in his travels, Paul's ministry in the city engendered a riot, and he was brought before the deputy on trumped-up charges, which were immediately dismissed because of Paul's practice of living as a law-abiding citizen unless the law directly contradicted his divine mission. (Acts 18:12-17) One interesting incident that occurred during his stay in Corinth was the vision in which the Lord assured the apostle that no harm would come to him in the city since "I [the Lord] have much people in this city." (Acts 18:10) The unusual aspect of that statement is that it came at the beginning of Paul's ministry there before there had been more than a handful of converts. In essence, this was a prophetic statement based on the foreknowledge and predetermined plan of God that there were many souls to be saved in the city. It seems that this revelation was also part of Paul's mission strategy – he believed that God had actually foreordained people to be part of His family. With that mentality, Paul could be aggressive in his evangelism and discipleship – going after the ones that God had already chosen. (Romans 8:29-31) After establishing a thriving church in this pagan seafront city, Paul left by boat with Aquila and Priscilla to Cenchrea (a harbor city that serviced trade routes into Italy and the rest of Europe) and then across the Aegean Sea to Ephesus (the largest city in the Roman Empire and a port city that was connected to all the major trade routes of the period) where he left the couple. It was in Ephesus that Aquila and Priscilla met Apollos – who later went to Corinth as the second pastor of the congregation there – and taught him the doctrine that they had learned from Paul. (Acts 18:19

and 26) After preaching at the local synagogue in Ephesus, Paul again set sail with intentions of going to Jerusalem for the feast; however, when he came to Caesarea (the Roman capital over Palestine), he briefly greeted the local believers and then traveled on to Antioch where the second journey ended. (Acts 18:18-22)

Third Missionary Journey

Paul stayed in Antioch for a while (Acts 18:23) before heading out on his third missionary journey, which began with a visit to Galatia and then Phrygia where he encouraged and strengthened the existing disciples. (Acts 18:23) Again, we can see a very significant element of his ministry strategy – exhortation and edification. (I Corinthians 14:12; Ephesians 2:20-21, 4:12; I Thessalonians 2:11; I Timothy 1:4) About the time that Apollos relocated to Corinth, Paul returned to Ephesus where he established himself for the next three years. (Acts 20:31) One of his first encounters there was with a dozen disciples of John the Baptist who had not heard the completion of the gospel story – the death and resurrection of Jesus and coming of the Holy Spirit. After Paul explained the rest of the story to them, these disciples believed the message, received baptism, and were filled with the Holy Spirit. (Acts 19:1-7) Paul then turned his attention to the synagogue where he preached for the next three months with apparently little acceptance. (Acts 19:8) He then began holding daily sessions in the school of Tyrannus – a course that ran for the next two years. (Acts 19:9-10) The end result of his persistent ministry and the work of those who had been trained under his teachings and empowered by the Holy Spirit is that "all who dwelt in Asia heard the word of the Lord Jesus, both Jews and Greeks." (Acts 19:10) In this ministry in Ephesus, we see another of the hallmarks of Paul's

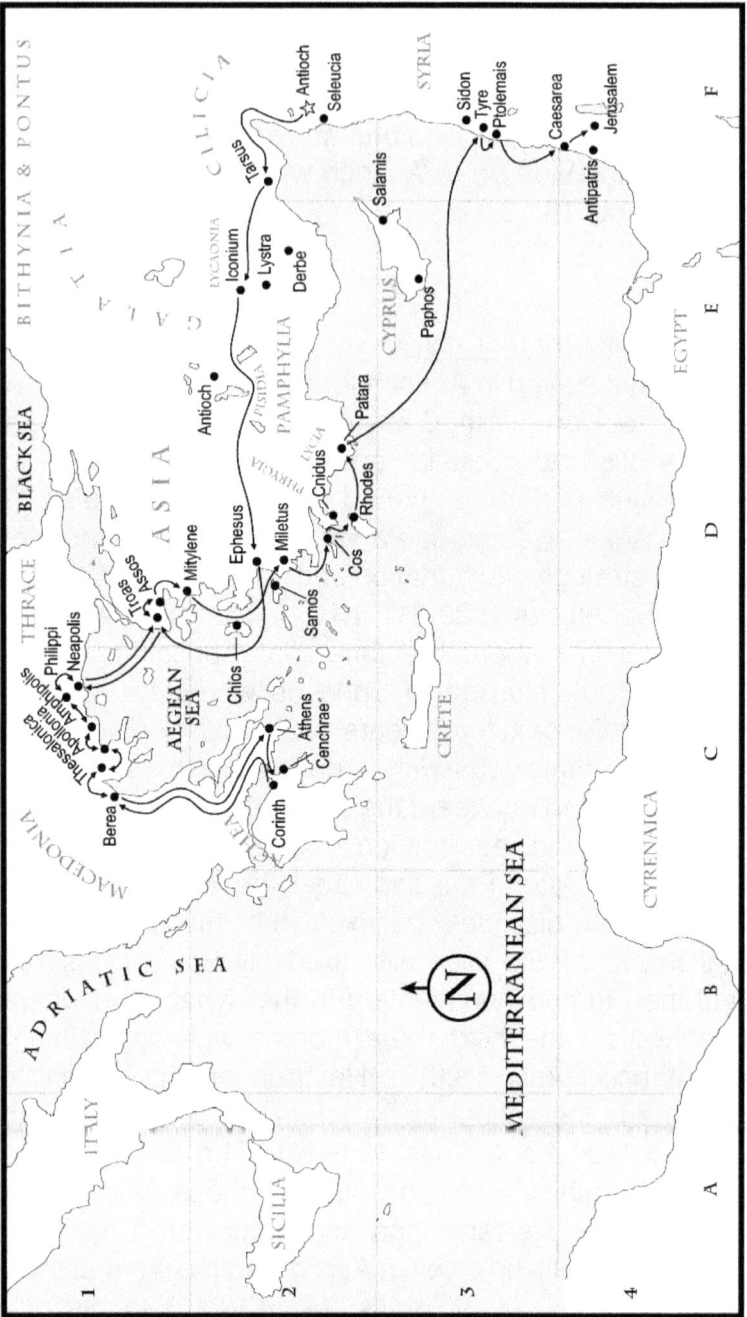

Paul's Third Mission Journey

ministry and message – the significance of the work of the Holy Spirit in the life of the believer. (Romans 8:4, 8:9, 8:13, 8:14, 8:26; Galatians 5:16, 5:22-23) In what would be called "power encounters" today, Paul brought about much change in the spiritual climate in Ephesus, with occult practitioners burning their books and the Temple of Diana – one of the Seven Wonders of the Ancient World that drew devotees from all over the then-known world – falling into near bankruptcy. (Acts 19:12-19, 19:23-41) The amazing thing is that Paul didn't protest these pagan practices; he simply preached the truth so strongly that the devil had to flee when the two forces collided – again, a benchmark of his ministry approach. (Romans 16:20; Ephesians 4:27, 6:11) On a side note, when I visited the city of Ephesus, I waited for the guide to point out the remains of the Temple of Diana. As we neared the end of the tour, he had still not mentioned this massive structure; so, I asked about it. He answered by asking if I remembered going past one particular stone several turns back. When I remarked that I did, he informed me that that was all that was left of the temple that was one of the Seven Wonders of the Ancient World. After pointing out site after site that had to do with Paul's time in the city, he had not even intended to mention the temple. Now that's what I call maximum impact!

It is likely that Paul wrote the letter to the Galatians while living in Ephesus. If this is the case, we can see another of the qualities that made Paul's ministry so impactful – he always had his converts on his heart and in his prayers. Paul sent Timothy and Erastus ahead into Macedonia, but he stayed in Ephesus (Acts 19:22) where he wrote I Corinthians (I Corinthians 16:8, 16:19) without the assistance of Timothy – whom he occasionally mentioned as an associate in other letters (Romans 16:21, II Corinthians 1:1, Philippians 1:1, Colossians 1:1, II Thessalonians 1:1, Philemon 1:1). Paul foresaw his route of travel for the next four or so years in Acts 19:21-22 – a strategy that agrees with the plans he spelled out to the believers in Corinth. (I Corinthians 16:1, 3, 5, 8-10) He wrote to the Corinthians about having a great and effectual door open for his ministry but that, at the same time, being faced by many adversaries (I Corinthians 16:9) – likely references to his effective ministry that led to the near bankruptcy of the Temple of Diana and the resulting mob violence at the amphitheater (Acts 19:23-41). After rejoining with Timothy (II Corinthians 1:1), Paul wrote a second letter to the Corinthians – possibly at Philippi – and traveled to Troas and Macedonia where he was joined by Titus (II Corinthians 2:12-13, 7:5-6, 7:13; Acts 20:1). At this point, there are two significant characteristics of Paul's ministry strategy that are obviously apparent – partnership and mentorship. Paul rarely traveled alone – possibly because of the safety factor, but more likely for the effectiveness factor of the synergism from partnership. (Ecclesiastes 4:8-12) The second aspect of his policy of traveling with men like Timothy and Titus was that he was constantly imparting into their lives so that they could absorb his passion, position, and purpose – the same thing that he communicated though letters to those who could not constantly travel with him.

After traveling through Macedonia in northern Greece, Paul arrived in Achaia in southern Greece where he spent the winter (Acts 20:2-3, I Corinthians 16:5-8) and wrote the book of Romans (Romans 15:23-26, I Corinthians 16:1-3). On their return trip to Macedonia (Acts 20:1), Paul and his team spent the Easter season in Philippi (Acts 20:6) and then set sail for Troas, where Paul preached an all-night sermon, resulting in Eutychus' falling out of the window and Paul's raising him from the dead (Acts 20:7-12). Paul then traveled into Turkey, stopping in Assos (home of the academy where Aristotle was chief to a group of philosophers and made innovative observations on zoology and biology), Mitylene (capital and port of the island of Lesbos and also the capital of the North Aegean Region), Chios (an island in the Aegean Sea), Samos (an especially rich and powerful city-state that was known for its vineyards and wine production), Trogylium (a stop-over point on the onward journey), and Miletus (once considered the greatest and wealthiest of Greek cities). Since he was unable to return to Ephesus at this time, he requested that the elders of the Ephesian church meet him in Miletus where he gave them what would be his farewell message. (Acts 20:16-38) From here, he sailed to Coos (most noted as the ancient home of Hippocrates the physician), Rhodes (capital of the group of islands in the region), and Patara (one of the principal cities of Lycia, the region's primary seaport, and a leading city of the Lycian League), and passed Cyprus to reach Tyre (the ancient Phoenician port city and the source of a highly valued purple dye used by royalty in the ancient world) where he and his traveling companions stayed a week before making their way through Ptolemais (capital of the province of Libya Superior or Libya Pentapolis) to Caesarea where they stayed many days (Acts 21:10) and finally ended their third journey in Jerusalem.

Arrest and Imprisonment

This visit to Jerusalem was to be a major turning point in Paul's life in that it would result in his arrest and eventual execution; however, these difficulties were not something that came to Paul unexpectedly. At numerous points during his journey toward the city, concerned believers warned him of impending danger. (Acts 20:23) At one point, the prophet Agabus physically tied the apostle up to demonstrate his destiny (Acts 21:10-12); however, Paul refused to be dissuaded by any of their pleadings because he knew from the Holy Spirit that what was ahead was part of God's plan for his life and ministry (Acts 20:22, 21:13-14). In fact, from

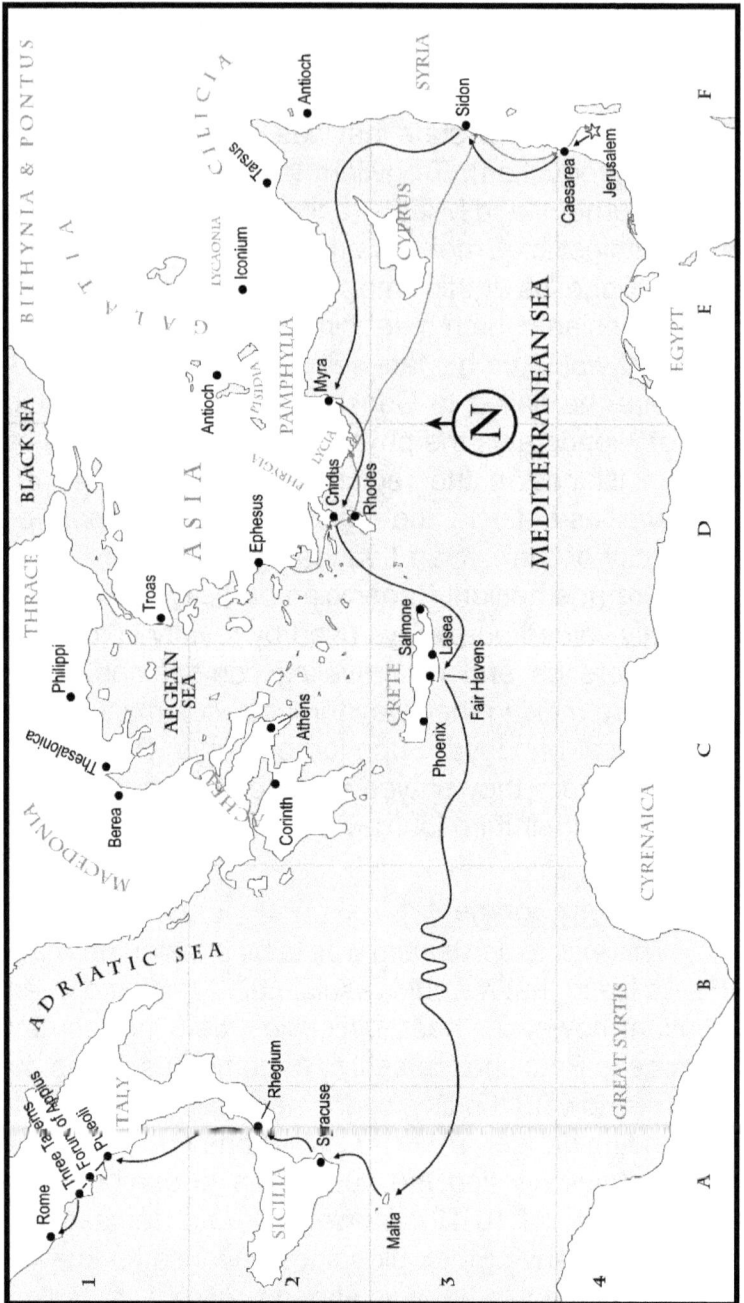

Paul's Fourth Mission Journey

day one of his Christian experience, Paul had been aware that his destiny included such sufferings. (Acts 9:16) Upon his arrival in the city, Paul met with James, the head elder in Jerusalem, who asked him to demonstrate that he had not forsaken the Jewish faith even though he was so outspoken about the liberty that gentiles had outside the regulations of the Jewish religion. Four Jewish Christian converts were to end a period of purification by participating in a Jewish ritual in the temple, and James felt that it would reaffirm Paul's validity among the Jewish background believers if he were to join them. (Acts 21:18-24) When Paul went into the temple, some Jews from Turkey saw him there and raised a clamor, yelling out that he was guilty of bringing a gentile into the court of the Jews. (Acts 21:27-29) The resulting riot was broken up by Roman soldiers who rushed from the Antonio Fortress and arrested Paul. (Acts 21:30-34) Amazing the Romans by the fact that he spoke Greek fluently, Paul requested permission to defend himself before the infuriated mob. When permission was given, he stopped partway up the stairs leading from the temple plaza to the Roman fortress and addressed the crowd in Hebrew (Acts 21:35-22:21) by simply sharing his testimony – a pattern that was characteristic of his defense speeches. When Paul mentioned his mission to the gentiles, such an uproar ensued that the soldiers dragged him into the fortress and would have beaten him except he appealed to his rights as a Roman citizen. This appeal led to the decision that Paul be transferred to the Sanhedrin for a hearing since there were obviously no legitimate charges that could be brought against him in a Roman court. (Acts 22:22-30) Knowing that the Sanhedrin was comprised of both Pharisees and Sadducees, Paul leveraged his position as a Pharisee to cause such internal distention between the two parties that the Romans had to intervene by pulling him out of the court and placing him under protective custody – the only thing they could do since he was a Roman citizen. When an assassination plot was uncovered, the Romans assigned a force of two officers, two hundred soldiers, seventy horsemen, and two hundred spearmen to escort Paul to the imperial headquarters at Caesarea – the first step to the fulfillment of a prophecy that the Lord had spoken to Paul during his Jerusalem incarceration, that he was to bear witness in Rome. (Acts 23:1-24)

As Paul was held in prison in Caesarea for the following two years, he had occasion to present his case before two Roman procurators (Felix and Festus) and the Jewish king Agrippa who would have released him except that Paul had exercised his right as a Roman citizen for his case to be heard as high up the chain of appeals as the emperor himself. (Acts 24:1-26:32) Paul was then taken as a prisoner under charge of a Roman centurion on commercial vessels on which civilians such as Luke and Aristarchus (Acts 27:1-2) could also book passage. The fateful journey was marked by a catastrophic storm in which the ship was destroyed – a situation what required the centurion to execute his prisoners on the spot rather than run the risk of their escape. However, because of Paul's favor with his captor and the fact that an angel had promised Paul that there would be no loss of life, the centurion defied protocol and spared the lives of his charges. (Acts 27:1-44) Finding themselves marooned on Melita (a small island south of Sicily) the castaways began to gather wood to build a fire to warm themselves. In what seemed to everyone who witnessed it be an act of divine judgment, Paul was bitten by a poisonous snake that was hiding in the driftwood that he collected – having escaped death at sea, judgment still loomed on the land. However, when Paul was unaffected by the strike of the venomous serpent, everyone immediately assumed that Paul must be a deity – the second time he has given this accolade. (Acts 28:1-6) The miracle opened the door for Paul to minster to the Roman official in charge of the island and to initiate a revival on the island where the survivors of the shipwreck spent the winter waiting for the opportunity to further their journey with the return of good weather the following spring. (Acts 28:7-11) The journey to Rome took them though Syracuse, Rhegium, and Puteoli where Paul was permitted to spend a week with some local believers. (Acts 28:12-14) Apparently, someone from here sent word ahead to Rome that Paul was being brought to the city, resulting in a company of believers coming to the Appii Forum to meet him and escort him onward to the city. (Acts 28:15) Once in Rome, Paul called the Jewish leaders together to explain the events surrounding his arrest and the actual lack of a case against him. Finding no consensus among the Jewish leaders, Paul remained in house arrest in the city for the following two years with seemingly unlimited freedom to teach and preach. (Acts 28:16-31) During this time he wrote Ephesians, Philippians, Colossians, and Philemon. Although there is no definitive proof of what happened to Paul after the open-ended close of the book of Acts, many Bible scholars assume that he was released from prison and had further missionary travels. If so, it was during this period that he wrote the epistles of Titus, I Timothy, and II Timothy. It is even likely that Paul may have fulfilled his desire to travel as far as Spain. (Romans 15:24, 15:28)

Missing Chapters

As we have taken this step-by-step journey through the life of Paul, we are aware that there are still missing chapters. In II Corinthians chapter eleven, Paul described many of the obstacles he endured during this journey: abundant labors, stripes too many to count, frequent imprisonments, repeated life-threatening situations, being beaten with whips to the Jewish legal limit times, being beaten with rods three times, three shipwrecks other than the one recorded in Acts chapter twenty-seven, suffering hypothermia from a night and a day treading water, being without food or water, and shivering in the cold without adequate clothing – all events that we are not sure where they fit into the storyline. In I Corinthians 15:32, he records having fought with wild beasts in Ephesus. This may be a symbolic reference to the amphitheater episode of Acts chapter nineteen, or it may be referring to a literal struggle against wild beasts – if so, here is another segment of the story that seems to remain untold.

Impact Strategies

Since everything that Paul did was an outward manifestation of the internal mission that was birthed in him on the road to Damascus, our journey through the apostle's life has helped us isolate a number of the things that caused his life to be one of maximum impact. Let's review these ministry strategies and see how they apply to not only his life but also to anyone who wishes to have maximum impact.

1) Picking strategic cities for his ministry

There is nothing inherently wrong with ministering in villages and rural areas – if that is where God has called you. However, maximum comes when the gospel penetrates the nerve center of a nation or culture. Dr. Lester Sumrall used to always say, "If you reach the major cities of a nation, you'll reach the whole nation because the major cities are like magnets drawing all the smart people from the villages. If they receive the gospel, they'll take it back to their villages when they go home to see Mamma!"

Even a cursory review of the notations made after the mention of all the cities Paul visited shows us that he never targeted the boondocks or backwater communities – not because the people there didn't need his gospel, but because he was determined to make maximum impact. Having grown up in Tarsus, which we know was "no mean city," and Jerusalem, the physical capital of the Jews and spiritual capital of the whole world – Paul was familiar with the significance of power centers. These political, cultural, business, educational, and religious centers of a nation attract the brightest minds, most adventurous spirits, and forward-thinking individuals who will launch out from these power bases to do business, spread ideas, and develop culture through their entire sphere of influence – including all the boondocks and backwater communities. Certainly it was because of this understanding that he recognized the necessity of preventing the gospel from reaching Damascus. He knew that it would be impossible to squelch the movement once it infected the bloodstream of the empire through the trade routes that interconnected in Damascus. Paul's conversion radically changed his theology – but not his methodology. Now, rather than taking the nip-it-in-the-bud approach, he saw the flip side of the coin – pollinate the power centers of the community so that they can then cross-pollinate and proliferate the gospel with maximum impact! Of course, the ultimate goal of this strategy was to infuse the gospel into Rome – the ultimate power base of the world – and from there to spread the seed of the gospel as far as Spain – the ultimate reachable limit of the world at that time. Significantly, even though Paul was not the first one to reach Rome with the gospel, he did give the church there an epistle in which he gave his finest expose of the gospel so that as they cross-pollinated the world they would do so with his DNA. Thus, he was able to make maximum impact – even before he personally set foot in the city!

2) Exercising of spiritual weapons to confront the forces of evil head-on and free the minds of men to hear and understand the gospel

A very prominent story comes from the life of my mentor Dr. Lester Sumrall, one of the great authorities on dealing with demonic power. When the Lord spoke to him to go to the Philippines to raise up a ministry there, He promised, "I will do more for you there than I have done for you anywhere else in your ministry." Knowing that there had never been any major Protestant revival in the Philippines in the history of the country and that there were very few Christians in the city, Bro. Sumrall went to Manila with great anticipation of what God was going to do. For the first several months, there was only a handful of people in his church. About the time that the congregation had grown to around fifty people, the Lord began impressing him that he was to build a barn to hold the coming harvest. So Bro. Sumrall started building a church that would seat twenty-five hundred people. He reasoned that he needed a building of at least that size since he had left a church in the US with over a thousand adults and a thousand children in the Sunday school each week, and the Lord had promised something bigger in the Philippines. Everybody begged him not to build such a large a facility. His denomination thought that he would make them the laughing stock of the entire world -- building a church to seat over two thousand when he only had fifty members. Protestant missionaries and prominent church leaders came to Manila to stop him because they were afraid he would take their members to fill his church. But he refused to be swayed by their arguments because he knew that God would bring a revival such as the Philippines had never seen.

One night as he was getting ready for bed, he and his wife listened to the evening news. Suddenly bloodcurdling screaming and horrifying howls come across the airwaves. The news feature was the story of a young girl incarcerated in the Bilibid Prison in Manila who had been mysteriously bitten by unseen teeth. Medical doctors and prison wardens observed as tooth marks and blood mysteriously appeared on her body. From his missionary experience, Bro. Sumrall recognized that this was demonic power tormenting her, so he got out of bed and lay on the floor praying and travailing, asking God to send somebody to deliver her from the demon power. But the Lord answered him, "If you don't do it, it won't happen. You are the only one in this city who knows how to cast the devil out of her." At that point, Bro. Sumrall had no way of knowing that what would happen with this girl was the key that would open up his ministry in the Philippines.

He spent that night in prayer and fasting. The next morning, he called the contractor building the church. Since he was a personal friend of the mayor, the contractor got Bro. Sumrall into the mayor's office where Bro. Sumrall asked for permission to go into the prison to pray for the girl. The story of the girl had already hit the international news, and the city had sent out appeals for church leaders, psychiatrists, or somebody to come and help her – but no one was able to deliver her. Bro. Sumrall went to pray for her, but he did not get a total victory the first day; so he went back again the second and third days. After three days of fasting and prayer he spoke to the spirit, and it left.   Not only was the girl set free, but a remarkable thing happened in the city. Unbeknownst to Bro. Sumrall, the demon spirit in that young girl was the principality spirit that ruled the entire Philippines. And as soon as its power was broken, the entire spirit realm of the Philippines became defenseless against the attack of the gospel.

When Bro. Sumrall was ushered back into the mayor's office with the good news that the girl had been freed, the mayor was so pleased that he asked what Bro. Sumrall wanted in return. His request was for permission to have large open-air revival meetings every night on the main plaza of the city. Within a six-week period, one hundred fifty thousand people were converted to Christ. When construction of the church was complete and the dedication service was held, the church was so jammed packed that most of the crowd could not get inside. This is the kind of results that come when a principality that is ruling over a geographic area is broken.

3) Ministering the gospel to people in positions of authority as a way of bringing its influence into a community from the top down

One phenomenal story that illustrates this point comes from the year 1956 when Tommy Hicks, a little-know evangelist was invited to Argentina. On the flight down, he was directed by the Holy Spirit to pray for a gentleman named "Juan Peron." It turned out that the Juan Peron he was to find and minister to was the presidential dictator of the country. When the evangelist showed up at the presidential palace to ask for permission to see the president, he was questioned as to what business he had trying to meet with President. Peron. When Hicks explained that he was there as a messenger from God with a gift of healing, the guard asked for prayer. Upon being instantly healed, the guard made arrangements for the evangelist to meet with the president, who was also miraculously healed as onlookers watched the healing manifest. The president granted Tommy Hicks permission to hold a healing crusade in the national soccer stadium and even came to the platform to testify of his healing. Argentina was rocked under the seismic impact of the Hicks' healing crusade.

4) Preaching to the Jews first as a way of starting with the religious community that already has some awareness of the scripture

This practice actually demonstrates two great principles of missionary evangelism – near cultural evangelism and looking for the "person of peace."

Near cultural evangelism is the process of ministering to a cultural group that has some similarity to your own but at the same time shares similarities with another group that may be totally alien to your background. I remember from my days of ministry on the campuses of secular colleges and universities that I had significant opportunities to minister to people in the drug culture during the days of the hippies who had "tuned in, turned on, and dropped out." Because I was able to connect with college students who had experimented with LSD and marijuana, they served as "go-betweens" to connect me with a culture that I could never have related to on my own.

Looking for the "person of peace" is a principle that Jesus taught His disciples when He sent them out on their first missionary adventure. "After these things the Lord appointed other seventy also, and sent them two and two before his face into every city and place, whither he himself would come. Therefore said he unto them, The harvest truly is great, but the labourers are few: pray ye therefore the Lord of the harvest, that he would send forth labourers into his harvest. Go your ways: behold, I send you forth as lambs among wolves. Carry neither purse, nor scrip, nor shoes: and salute no man by the way. And into whatsoever house ye enter, first say, Peace be to this house. And if the son of peace be there, your peace shall rest upon it: if not, it shall turn to you again. And in the same house remain, eating and drinking such things as they give: for the labourer is worthy of his hire. Go not from house to house." (Luke 10:1-7)

Notice that the passage we so often quote in context of raising up missionaries and evangelists, "The harvest truly is great, but the labourers are few: pray ye therefore the Lord of the harvest, that he would send forth labourers into his harvest," is right in the center of His directive for the disciples to go out on their mission. He was not sending them to the churches where they could recruit evangelists and missionaries, but to places where He had not yet been – to the mission field itself. Perhaps we have too often isolated this message from its context and have, therefore, missed the major emphasis of Jesus' words. As the disciples were to go out to minister, they were directed to be in constant prayer for someone else to be raised up to continue the ministry. The disciples were not to go out with the anticipation of bringing in the harvest singlehandedly, rather, they were to go out with the anticipation of seeing other harvesters raised up. In other words, they were to expect that they would duplicate themselves through their mission. Next they were not to anticipate bringing in huge harvests as much as they were to look for some specific individuals whom Jesus labeled as the sons of peace in each community. Once they found these specific individuals, they were to enter into their homes and not wander around the neighborhood. In essence, they were to settle in on one individual household and invest in that home the way Jesus had invested in them—eating, sleeping, working, playing, laughing, and crying with them – until the knowledge of the kingdom of God that was inside those individuals was brought to full fruition. I'm certain that this approach did not preclude them from doing mass evangelism any more than Jesus had to give up ministering to the multitudes in order to disciple His chosen twelve. If we look into the life of Paul, we see this pattern at work when he focused on Lydia's household while ministering to the whole city of Philippi and when he joined in with Aquila and Priscilla in their tent making business while ministering to the whole city of Corinth. When Paul entered Corinth, the Lord spoke to him that He had "much people" in the city. (Acts 18:10) This revelation came before the city was evangelized, indicating that there were many sons and daughters of peace in the city waiting to be revealed.

Jesus' intent was for us to disciple the nations. Our first focus should be to find a son or daughter of peace in the area and begin to invest our lives in that individual and his or her family. The biblical example was to essentially move in with the family. In most cultures today, this would not be practical; however, we need to make ourselves totally available and totally vulnerable to this son or daughter of peace and his or her family. Essentially, we are to instill into them who we are as much as what we believe. Paul wrote of Timothy, saying that he had fully known his doctrine and his manner of life. (II Timothy 3:10) Raising up believers is not just a matter of teaching them what we know, but also letting them know what we are. The end goal would be that we could say to them as Jesus said to His disciples, "He that hath seen me hath seen the Father." (John 14:9)

The Bible gives a few hints as to how we are to recognize sons and daughters of peace when we encounter them. Jesus recognized Nathanael as a son of peace as soon as He saw him under a fig tree. (John 1:47-50) The significance of this illustration is that the Jewish rabbis made a practice of sending their students to do their recitations under a fig tree. Apparently, Nathaniel was studying the scripture when Jesus first noticed him. The fact that Nicodemus risked his reputation as a leader in the established religion of the day by coming to see Jesus secretly at night proved that he was sincerely seeking the kingdom of God—proof that he was a true son of peace. (John 3:1-2) When Jesus came upon the woman at the well (John 4:4-26), He identified her as a daughter of peace who would immediately spread the message to all the men of Samaria (verses 27-42). The very fact that this woman continued to bounce from man to man even though it had cost her her reputation and acceptability in the city proved that she was desperate for love and would not stop looking no matter how much her quest would cost her. Jesus understood that it was more than just physical love she needed; she was on a quest for divine love because the kingdom of God was already trying to invade her heart. In Luke 9:57-62, we read the story of three individuals who volunteered to join the disciples but were not accepted because they were not sons of peace. In each case, Jesus could see that they had other kingdoms established in their hearts. Whether it was money, family, or any other earthly pursuit, their self-absorbed motivations disqualified these men from being sons of peace and, therefore, candidates for discipleship. Certainly, it was because Jesus only focused His discipleship efforts on those individuals who truly displayed the qualities of sons of peace that He was able to say at the end of His ministry that all except one of them were faithfully preserved in the faith. (John 17:12) When the multitude turned away from Jesus because they felt that His teachings were too difficult, the true disciples stayed because they realized that no one else had word of life, a solid indicator that they were sons of peace. (John 6:60-71)

These sons and daughters of peace may come from any walk of life. As we have already noted, there could be blue-collar workers (Aquila and Priscilla), business owners (Lydia), religious leaders (Paul), social outcasts (the woman at the well), political leaders (Publius), beauty queens (Esther), and wealthy socialites (Barnabas). We can easily add to that list IRS agents (Matthew and Zacchaeus), housewives (Mary and Martha), students (Daniel and Samuel), ranchers (David and Moses), fishermen (Peter, James, and John), and any other position in life—including yours!

5) Being willing to put his own life on the line for the gospel

When I first visited South Korea, I was amazed at the number of churches I saw in the country; there seemed to be a building with a cross on the front or roof on every corner. I was especially impacted by this ubiquitous presence of the faith after having traveled in other Asian countries where Christianity was essentially nonexistent. But there is a story behind the entry of the gospel into the country. In 1866, Robert Thomas sailed into the mouth of the Taedong River with cases of Bibles in the Korean language. In an attempt to stop the entry of the gospel, the Koreans set his boat afire. In the midst of the roaring flames, Thomas began to unpack the Bibles and toss them to shore – even as his own clothing burst into flames. Engulfed in the inferno of the sinking ship, he continued to sow the seed of the Word of God into the unwelcoming soil. When he eventually lept from the ship and was arrested, he continued to distribute the Bibles to those who arrested, tried, and executed him. The end of the story is that some of the Bibles were used as material for wallpapering in the home of one of the official. As curious guests began to read the writings on the wall, revival came to the land.

6) Demonstrating the gospel with healings and signs and wonders

Throughout the history of the Christian church, the gospel has always been spread most effectively when signs and wonders accompanied the preaching of the Word. After all, that was Jesus' original plan. (Mark 16:17-18) But let me share just one story from contemporary history to illustrate the point. T.L. Osborn first went to India as an on-fire and determined missionary; however, he soon realized that he lacked something necessary to reach the unbelievers of India. When he discovered that the Muslims believed in one God and had a book that they held as scared as the Christians do their Bible, he was was totally disillusioned and slipped away from the mission compound in the dead of night. "With his tail tucked between his hind legs," he returned to the USA and began to question if he could ever be a missionary and have an impact among unbelievers. However, all that changed in one night when he sat in the upper balcony at a healing crusade directed by William Braham. As miracle after miracle occurred on the main platform, the Holy Spirit spoke to T.L., "You can do THAT! You can DO that! You CAN do that! YOU can do that!" After receiving the empowerment of the Holy Spirit, T.L. and his wife Daisy returned to the mission field and over the course of the next five decades traveled to more than seventy countries and reached millions of people in crusades that often numbered into the tens of thousands in attendance. Every meeting was accompanied by miracles of biblical proportions. They created prolific quantities of evangelistic and training materials, some of which were translated into more than one hundred thirty languages. Under his influence, more than one hundred fifty thousand churches were birthed.

7) Praising in the midst of trouble as the way to open doors of deliverance

For an illustration of this principle, let me take you to the earliest historical record of the Christian faith – the records of Eusibius, the first person to chronical the movement.

I myself saw some of these mass executions by decapitation or fire, a slaughter that dulled the murderous axe until it wore out and broke in pieces, while the executioners grew so tired they had to work in shifts. But I also observed a marvelous eagerness and a divine power and enthusiasm in those who placed their faith in Christ; as soon as the first was sentenced, others would jump up on the tribunal in front of the judge and confess themselves Christians. Heedless of torture in its terrifying forms but boldly proclaiming their devotion to the God of the universe, they received the final sentence of death with joy, laughter, and gladness, singing hymns of thanksgiving to God until their last breath.

8) Obeying the civil authorities

This item might seem a bit foreign to us was Paul's insistence on living according the laws of the land – even though the government might be hostile to the gospel. In fact, he even defined the government officials as ministers of God. (Romans 13:4) When Paul was arrested and threatened with beating, he took advantage of every right and privilege he had as a Roman citizen. (Acts 22:25) When there was a conspiracy against his life, Paul used his status under the Roman legal system for his protection. (Acts 23:17) When he realized that extradition to Jerusalem would seal his doom, the apostle exercised his legal right of appeal to ensure that he not fall into the deathtrap set for him by the Jewish officials. (Acts 25:11) So, we see that Paul did not see himself as an enemy of the state or the state as his adversary. In fact, even when the government had imprisoned him and was ready to execute him, Paul seemed to say that even their act of killing him would be a fulfillment of God's will and, therefore, a blessing to him. (Philippians 1:21) He even served as a divine advisor to the government on at least one occasion (Acts 27:9-10); even though they refused his advice, they soon discovered that his instructions were beneficial and crucial to their very lives (Acts 27:21-44). Because Paul held no malice against the Roman government even though they were oppressing and persecuting believers, he was able to receive benefits from the government and give his blessing to it.

Throughout church history, there have been times when the governments were hostile to the faith – as I have just mentioned. However, when it has been possible to find a common ground, that acceptance has amplified the growth of the church. One example can be found in the introduction of the faith into the Britain. In AD 596, Augustine and forty Benedictine monks were commissioned to go to England as missionaries. Due to diseases and hostilities along the way, only seven of the monks actually reached the English Channel and the British Isles; however, their mission met with even more opposition when they attempted to witness to King Ethelbert. Fortunately, his wife was a Christian, and she eventually persuaded him to be converted. Upon the king's profession of faith, Christianity became the official religion of the country and ten thousand new converts were baptized in one day.

9) Caring for the churches

Paul was consumed with his love for the churches. Reading the introductions to his letters gives us a glimpse into his never-ending concern for the saints. To the Corinthians, he wrote, "I thank my God always on your behalf." To the Philippians, he said, "I thank my God upon every remembrance of you." He addressed the Colossians, "We give thanks to God and the Father of our Lord Jesus Christ, praying always for you." His greeting to the

Thessalonian church read, "We give thanks to God always for you all, making mention of you in our prayers." Timothy he addressed as "my own son in the faith" and "my dearly beloved son" and went on to say, "I thank God, whom I serve from my forefathers with pure conscience, that without ceasing I have remembrance of thee in my prayers night and day." Titus also received the loving salutation of "mine own son after the common faith." In writing to Philemon, Paul also addressed Apphia whom he called "beloved" and then wrote, "I thank my God, making mention of thee always in my prayers." From these opening lines, we are able to get a glimpse inside the heart of the great Christian leader. His converts were never out of his heart and mind. No matter how many miles and how many years separated them, these loved ones were always in Paul's prayers. But it is in his greeting to the church at Rome that we are able to really see what is in the heart of this great minister of God. These believers he addressed as "beloved" even though he did not personally know them. They were part of the Body of Christ, so he loved them intently – even without a direct relationship. Paul had a heart of unceasing love and concern for the Body of Christ, whether personal friend or total stranger. In II Corinthians chapter eleven, Paul graphically illustrated how heavily the burden of love for the church weighed upon his heart. Here, he described the physical difficulties he endured for the gospel's sake. beatings, imprisonments, shipwrecks, long journeys, plots against his life, attacks of wild beasts, assaults by robbers, hunger, exposure, and being stoned to the point of death. Yet he concluded this list with, "Beside those things that are without, that which cometh upon me daily, the care of all the churches." (verse 28) Here he seems to say that the inner burden he carried for the churches exceeded the physical burdens that had been hurled upon him externally.

Perhaps the biggest movement in the Body of Christ in the world today is among the underground churches of China. Although little is reported to the outside world because of the security issues involved and the need to protect the believers, the accounts that I have heard seem to indicate that the reason for the growth is an elaborate system of internal care for one another. One leader of the underground movement that I had the privilege of meeting described to me how that he kept personal contact with the pastors of over four hundred house churches and that each of these pastors had similar numbers of other house churches that they also cared for. Because they are careful that no one "falls through the cracks," they are able to keep the pastors strong in the faith and accurate in their doctrine. These pastors, in turn, care for the spiritual and physical needs of their parishioners. In such an environment of love and healthy oversight, the churches are experiencing exponential growth.

10) Mentoring disciples

Mentoring and discipling individuals in the faith one at a time may seem to be a slow process by which to win the world to Jesus. However, if done purposefully and consistently, it can be the most powerful force imaginable in world evangelism. If you could win one thousand people per year to Jesus every year for seventeen years, you would have brought seventeen thousand individuals into the kingdom of God during your lifetime of ministry.

However, if you were able to win one person every six months and disciple these new converts and teach them to also win a new convert every six months, the exponential growth of your evangelism would be that of reaching more than the world's population in the same amount of time. This is the power of exponential growth. In addition, it is a cure for the classic evangelistic approach that has rendered much of mission work subject to the mile-wide-but-inch-deep syndrome.

One classic example of this simple, but powerful, multiplication principle was demonstrated when the game of chess was first invented. When the creator of the game showed his invention to the ruler of the country, the king was so pleased that he gave the inventor the right to name his prize for the invention. The man requested that one grain of rice be placed on the first square of the chessboard, two grains on the second square, four on the third square, and so forth, doubling the amount each time he moved to the next square. The ruler, mathematically naive, quickly accepted the inventor's offer, even getting offended by his perceived notion that the inventor was asking for such a seemingly low price. He ordered the treasurer to count and hand over the rice to the inventor. However, when the treasurer took more than a week to calculate the amount of rice needed, the ruler asked him for a reason for his tardiness. The treasurer then gave him the result of the calculation and explained that it would be impossible to give the inventor the reward – more than eighteen quintillion grains of rice, exceeding the world's total output. Talk about maximum impact!

This is the same model that God used to populate the earth in the first place. The entire world's physical population came from one family; not one man having many children, but each child having his own children. Impacting nations works exactly the same way – through bringing converts to the state of maturity where they are able to reproduce themselves in the lives of others who will in turn perpetuate the process. Add this reproductive growth to the results gained through evangelism, and the gospel becomes an unstoppable force in the world!

11) Being filled with Holy Spirit

In order to impact the world for Jesus, it is absolutely mandatory that we be filled and led by the Holy Spirit. (Luke 24:49, Acts 1:4) If we don't have His direction is our evangelism, we will never be able to supernaturally deal with situations that are actually controlled in the spiritual dimension even though they are present in the physical realm. Let me share one simple story that can help illustrate how this principle works. When I was serving as a chaplain in Yosemite National Park, I had to hold down a secular job in order to be permitted to live in the park. One summer, I worked as a waiter in one of the restaurants. My supervisor was a young lady about my same age. She was attractive and smart, but there was just one problem – she "cussed like a sailor." I felt that I should be able to do something to help her conquer this problem, but I had no idea what to do. As I prayed about the situation, I received an idea that I knew unquestionably was the Holy Spirit showing me how to deal with the issue. The Holy Spirit said, "I'm going to tell you what to say, and I'm going to tell you when to say it." At that point, I received one simple sentence. I carried that sentence around in my heart for the next couple of weeks waiting for the time when the Holy Spirit wanted me to say it. Then it happened! One day, during a very busy dinner hour in the restaurant, a waiter was bringing a full tray of food out of the kitchen and a busboy was carrying an equally full tray of dirty dishes back to be washed. Somehow, they collided at the swinging door between the kitchen and the dining room. Crystal shattered, china crashed, silverware clanged, food splattered everywhere! I'll always remember a roast duck sliding across the entire length of the dining hall floor. It turned out that I was just a couple steps away from the scene and my supervisor was about the same distance on the other side of the mess; therefore, we arrived at the same second. Instantly, the Holy Spirit said, "Now!" Before she could open her mouth to scold her errant employees, I blurted out, "Debbie, you are too beautiful a person to say what's about to come out of your mouth." The collision between the two servers was mild compared to the impact that that one sentence had on her! She lost seventy-five percent of her vocabulary in that split second, and the worst thing that I heard come out of her mouth the rest of that summer was, "Gosh." That is the kind of impact that we want our lives to have.

12) Partnering with other believers

One problem that continually plagues the Body of Christ is the tendency to think that we can do everything on our own – even though the Bible specifically instructs us that we are to see ourselves as members of a large body with each member supplying a necessary part. (I Corinthians 12:12-21, Ephesians 4:16) I heard of an excellent illustration of this point that occurred in a so-called closed country. There was a lady missionary working there who was well-versed in the scripture, trained in cross-cultural communication, and knew the language and customs of the people. In other words, she should have been the "poster boy" (or girl) of success in the country. However, after several years, her work had been totally unproductive. It was when she had just about reached the point of giving up that she met someone from a Christian ministry that had been broadcasting radio programing into her nation. They had files filled with names and addresses of people from that country that had responded to their broadcasts but no way to follow up on them. When they released those files to the missionary, she began to contact the seekers and planted sixteen churches in less than a year.   Neither the missionary nor the broadcasting company was having maximum impact until they partnered together.

13) Following God's directions – even if they lead into danger

There are probably no better examples than the testimonies of Jim and Elizabeth Elliot. Jim's first missionary exposure was linguistic studies with the Wycliffe translators. It was here that he first learned of the Huaorani (also called the "Auca," the Quichua word for "savage"), a group of Ecuadorian indigenous people considered violent and dangerous to outsiders.   Although many friends and family members encouraged him to use his skills as a youth pastor in the US, Jim considering the home church "well-fed" and determined that international missions should take precedence.   Jim and four other missionaries – Ed McCully, Roger Youderian, Pete Fleming, and their pilot, Nate Saint – dedicated their lives to reaching these isolated tribal groups. They first made contact with the Huarani from their Piper

PA-14 airplane using a loudspeaker and a basket to pass down gifts. After several months, the men decided to make physical contact with the Huaorani by landing their plane on a little strip of beach along the Curaray River not far from their village. There they were approached one time by a small group of Huaorani and even gave an airplane ride to one curious Huaorani whom they called "George" (his real name was Naenkiwi). Encouraged by these friendly encounters, they began plans to visit the Huaorani, without knowing that Naenkiwi had lied to the others about the missionaries' intentions. Even though Jim carried a gun with him, he had determined that it would only be used to fire warning shots to scare off any attackers. When a group of Huaorani warriors did attack, Jim did not defend himself and the entire missionary party was speared to death on January 8, 1956.

His journal entry for October 28, 1949, expresses his belief that work dedicated to Jesus was more important than his life, "He is no fool who parts with that which he cannot keep, when he is sure to be recompensed with that which he cannot lose."

Even though Jim died in his attempt to reach the Huaorani people with the gospel, the true heart for the nations was demonstrated by Elizabeth when she took their young daughter and moved to the village of the very people who killed her husband and lived with them for a number of years until the tribe (including the assassins who took her husband's life) came to Christ.

14) Standing up for what is right while endeavoring to keep the spirit of unity in bond of peace without compromising (Ephesians 4:3) – an incredible

accomplishment for Paul at the Jerusalem Council concerning circumcision

The story of William Carey is one of the greatest stories of maximum impact – something that would never have happened had he not been able to stand up against the erroneous ideas of the church leadership of his day with conviction yet in a way that preserved the unity of the spirit in the bond of peace. At a time when the Protestant churches of Europe and the Americas had no vision for foreign missions, Carey spoke boldly to convince the Western Church to send missionaries to the unreached world, to share the gospel with the non-Christians of India, and to convince the government to make powerful social changes in the culture.

Before becoming a recoginized church leader, Carey spent his hours as he mended shoes at his cobbler's bench praying over a world map that he had posted on the wall. By 1787, he became so burdened for the lost of the world that he approached the British Baptist Association with the question of whether it was the duty of all Christians to spread the gospel. The retort that came back was, "Young man, sit down; when God pleases to convert the heathen, he will do it without your aid and mine." However, after persistent persuasion and the presentation of his groundbreaking missionary manifesto <u>An Enquiry into the Obligations of Christians to Use Means for the Conversion of the Heathens</u>, Carey was commissioned as the first Protestant foreign missionary in 1792 and became known as the Father of Modern Protestant Missions. As soon as funds were raised, he set sail for Calcutta, India, where he invested the rest of his life. Although he and his team produced only about seven hundred converts, they left behind a legacy of a transformed India by: translating the Bible into thirty-four Asian languages; compiling dictionaries of Sanskrit, Marathi, Panjabi, and Telegu; founding the still influential Serampore College; establishing churches and nineteen mission stations; planting more than one hundred rural schools; encouraging the education of girls; starting the Horticultural Society of India; serving as a professor at Fort William College; began the weekly publication The Friend of India; printing the first Indian newspaper; introducing the concept of the savings bank to assist poor farmers; fighting against sati, the burning of widows; and much more. He had maximum impact not only on the mission field but also on the Protestant church in that he actually birthed the modern missions movement that has changed the whole world in the past two centuries.

15) Refused to take credit for healing

In the early twentieth century, a British evangelist rose to prominence because of the remarkable healing that occurred in his crusades. Unfortunately, at the height of his ministry, he made one boastful statement in a massive campaign in Africa. Gazing across the thousands who had gathered to hear him preach, he proclaimed, "The whole world is at my feet!" Within weeks after that statement, he was stricken with the same debilitating disease that he had set literally hundreds of sufferers free from in his public ministry. He was on his way to having maximum impact, but sabotaged his own career and the lives of all those whom he could have reached.

The Testimonies of Those Whom Paul's Life Impacted

Obviously, the task of exploring the impact that Paul had on the lives of the individuals he touched during his lifetime would take us far beyond the limits of just one volume; therefore, I'd like to look at just two examples – one individual and one congregation. For the individual, I'd like to choose Paul's closest friend – and likely the most abundant recipient of his spiritual DNA – his disciple Timothy, a young man whom he chose to mentor and groom for the kingdom of God. For the congregation, I'd like to select the church at Thessalonica – an outstanding example of the maximum impact of Paul's life and ministry in that, as we have already noted, he was able to establish a viable church even in adverse conditions during a short three-week visit.

Timothy

The story of how Paul selected Timothy is recorded in the sixteenth chapter of Acts – which, as we have already observed, immediately followed the council in Jerusalem in which Paul played a major role in helping the early church leaders come to the conclusion that it was unnecessary for gentile converts to receive the ritual of circumcision – a major tradition for Jews and anyone who would desire to convert to Judaism. Although Timothy was Jewish from his mother's side of the family, he was Greek from his father's side of the family and had, therefore, not been circumcised as a newborn. When Paul selected Timothy to become his traveling companion, he decided that his young companion should be circumcised so as to defuse any challenges that might arise against him. Although he had just fought a valent battle to win liberty for his converts, Paul felt it necessary to set a high standard in the life of this one individual – likely because he knew that Timothy was destined for a very significant role in his own life and in the establishment of the church. In other words, Paul set the bar high so that he could obtain Olympic-quality performance from this unique man. And world-class results did come out of the relationship between Paul and Timothy. In fact, Paul described Timothy with unparalleled accolades, "I have no man likeminded, who will naturally care for your state. For all seek their own, not the things which are Jesus Christ's. But ye know the proof of him, that, as a son with the father, he hath served with me in the gospel." (Philippians 2:20-22)

Based on the close relationship and single-heartedness between Paul and his protégé, we can likely gain some significant insight into the man and ministry of Paul by examining what it was that Paul imparted into him – the premier product of his ministry. In one of the personal letters that the apostle wrote to his disciple, Paul gave us an articulate list of the aspects of his life and character that he had invested into his young disciple.

> But thou hast fully known my doctrine,
> manner of life, purpose, faith, longsuffering,
> charity, patience, Persecutions, afflictions,
> which came unto me at Antioch, at Iconium,
> at Lystra; what persecutions I endured: but
> out of them all the Lord delivered me. (II
> Timothy 3:10-11)

Let's use the apostle's own outline as an approach to understanding who this man really was. Since these were the aspects of his life that he felt had most significantly shaped Timothy, they were obviously the major traits that defined the man and ministry that has had maximum impact in the history of the world we live in.

Doctrine

The first item Paul mentioned that he saw as a determining factor in impacting Timothy's life was his doctrine. Obviously, the theological teaching of the Apostle Paul is a subject that could fill libraries; therefore, it is a subject beyond the scope of one simple manuscript. Fortunately, we have a three distilled versions of his teachings available in the New Testament – Romans and the companion volumes of Colossians and Ephesians. The New Testament is not a theology book, although it is the only reliable book on theology. When I say that it is not a theology book, I am intending to say that it is not a systematic study of theology. Rather it is a book of applied theology; it is a practical application of theology to the everyday problems of life. For example, Paul did not write the book of Galatians to impart theological lessons to the believers in Galatia but to correct errors and misconceptions in their church. In doing so, he had to explain a lot of theology along the way.

The most significant time when Paul did put quill to parchment in a theological statement was when he penned the epistle to the Romans. This church was not one he had founded; since he was not involved in their lives like he was in the other churches, he could not speak to them in the corrective tone with which he addressed other congregations. To the Romans, he imparted his spiritual gift of teaching in a more methodical manner by laying out a systematic explanation of the theology of salvation. Interestingly enough, he gave a condensed version of this same theology in chapter two of the book of Ephesians and an even more condensed synopsis in the first chapter of the letter to the Colossians. In writing to the Romans, Paul made reference to his desire to visit them and impart a gift to them so that they would be established. (Romans 1:11) After consideration of all the possibilities of what it could have been that he planned to give to these fellow believers, the most apparent possibility is that he wanted to leave them with a clear understanding of the doctrine of Christ. This is exactly what his epistle to the Romans is – a full systematic treatise on the theology of salvation, explaining that all men are sinners, that God has made a plan for salvation and complete restoration for man, that the Holy Spirit is the power of the Christian life, and that certain responses are required on man's part. In this, the book of Romans stands apart from Paul's other writings. Since he was not correcting their behavior or theology, he took the opportunity to write to them about the comprehension he had of what was essential to the gospel.

In the first chapter of Romans, Paul established the fact that God has revealed Himself to mankind, but it is man's attitude toward Him that determines how they will experience God, "For therein is the righteousness of God revealed from faith to faith: as it is written, The just shall live by faith. For the wrath of God is revealed from heaven against all ungodliness and unrighteousness of men, who hold the truth in unrighteousness." (Romans 1:17-18) He went on that say that all the depravity in the human condition is a result of men's refusing to pursue a proper acknowledgment of God, "When they knew God, they glorified him not as God, neither were thankful; but became vain in their imaginations, and their foolish heart was darkened. Professing themselves to be wise, they became fools, And changed the glory of the uncorruptible God into an image made like to corruptible man, and to birds, and to fourfooted beasts, and creeping things. Wherefore God also gave them up to uncleanness through the lusts of their own hearts, to dishonour their own bodies between themselves: Who changed the truth of God into a lie, and worshipped and served the creature more than the Creator, who is blessed for ever." (Romans 1:21-25) In chapter two,

Paul focused on the gentile nations who do not have the written revelation of God in the Old Testament as do the Jewish people. He concluded that they are guilty of violating the natural revelation given to them even though they don't have the codified law of God to guide them, "For as many as have sinned without law shall also perish without law: and as many as have sinned in the law shall be judged by the law." (Romans 2:12) In the second half of the chapter, the apostle turned his attention to the Jews who had the explicit law of God to follow. In doing so, Paul summarized that they, too, were guilty of sin before God because they did not follow the law even though they had it tangibly with them, "Thou that makest thy boast of the law, through breaking the law dishonourest thou God." (Romans 2:23) In chapter three, Paul wrapped up his discussion of sin by declaring that everyone is guilty, "For all have sinned, and come short of the glory of God." (Romans 3:23) However, in the same breath, he presented the hopeful message of the gospel that human sinfulness has been overcome through the gracious gift of forgiveness that is not dependent upon human achievement but upon God's free gift through faith in Jesus, "But now the righteousness of God without the law is manifested, being witnessed by the law and the prophets; Even the righteousness of God which is by faith of Jesus Christ unto all and upon all them that believe...Being justified freely by his grace through the redemption that is in Christ Jesus." (Romans 3:21-24) Paul then introduced such theological concepts as justification (Romans 5:9), reconciliation (Romans 5:10), and atonement (Romans 5:11) to explain the salvation process. In chapter six Paul centered the discussion around the sacrament of baptism as a physical object lesson of the transformation that occurs in the salvation experience, "We are buried with him by baptism into death: that like as Christ was raised up from the dead by the glory of the Father, even so we also should walk in newness of life." (Romans 6:4) In chapter seven, the apostle grappled with the question of why we sometimes don't see the practical transformation that we know has spiritually occurred in accepting salvation by grace through faith, "For I delight in the law of God after the inward man: But I see another law in my members, warring against the law of my mind, and bringing me into captivity to the law of sin which is in my members." (Romans 7:22-23) But it is in chapter eight that Paul answered the questions he raised in chapter seven – it is only through the power of the Holy Spirit in the life of a believer that he can ever manifest his inner spiritual transformation in his practical life, "The law of the Spirit of life in Christ Jesus hath made me free from the law of sin and death. For what the law could not do, in that it was weak through the flesh, God sending his own Son in the likeness of sinful flesh, and for sin, condemned sin in the flesh: That the righteousness of the law might be fulfilled in us, who walk not after the flesh, but after the Spirit." (Romans 8:2-4) In chapters nine through fifteen, the apostle addressed issues that exemplify how this spiritual transformation is to be walked out in the practical world; and in chapter sixteen, he concluded with some personal notes and the promise that there is soon to come a final resolution to the whole spiritual battle that is raging in human hearts, society, and history, "The God of peace shall bruise Satan under your feet shortly. The grace of our Lord Jesus Christ be with you. Amen." (Romans 16:20)

The other concise presentations of Paul's doctrine are the companion epistles of Ephesians and Colossians. Even a cursory overview of the two letters reveals that Colossians is very similar to Ephesians. This similarity has led Bible students to surmise that it is likely that the two were written at about the same time and may have even been based on the same outline — at least the same mental outline, if not the same physical outline. But before we can see exactly what these books reveal about Paul's theology, we need to do a bit of background analysis. When compared to the way most of his letters give point-blank advice to specific issues in the churches, it is readily observable that the Ephesian letter has a rather unique generalized tone. Because of this general terminology coupled with the fact that the very earliest copies of the letter to the Ephesians do not include the word "Ephesians" in the title, many Bible scholars have concluded that Paul had intended the letter for a much wider audience than just one church. It is likely that the copies that do say "Ephesians" were from the copy of the circular letter that was actually sent to that specific city while other copies went to other churches in the same general area, perhaps the seven churches of Asia Minor mentioned in Revelation chapters two and three. Based on references in Colossians about another letter that had been sent to the Laodicean church, some scholars have gone so far as to suggest that Colossians was also a circular letter that was to be passed between the two churches of Colossi and Laodicea, if not all the churches in Asia Minor. It is an intriguing idea to consider that this "Laodicean letter" may have even been the untitled version of the letter we now know as Ephesians.

In a previous section, we have alluded to the fact that these letters were likely written during Paul's imprisonment in Rome. If this suggestion is correct, then they are some of the last works of the apostle. This chronology places the letters late in his life, meaning that these letters give us the full benefit of his total spiritual maturity. Although Paul came to a comprehensive revelation of the gospel during his sojourn in Arabia, he did have experiences that matured him throughout his lifetime – one example can be seen in the experience in Athens that we will discuss in a later section. If his ministry approach changed so significantly on that short episode of his life, imagine how much more seasoned he must have been by the time he came to those last few years and stood poised at the very portal of heaven.

If these letters were indeed circular letters, there is a certain richness to them that will not be found in the more where-the-rubber-meets-the-road letters like the Corinthian epistles and the letter to the Galatians in which he offers more practical counsel concerning specific issues. In the Corinthian correspondence, for example, the church members had sent him a list of questions that he enumerated and then addressed. (I Corinthians 7:1-16:18) In the Ephesian and Colossian letters, he is not addressing any specific issues; therefore, he is able to give in-depth revelation concerning the main issue — who Christ is in us and who we are in Him! Furthermore, if indeed these missives were circular letters that were associated with Ephesus and Laodicea, we have a parallel with the book of Revelation. Ephesus was the first church addressed, and Laodecia was the last. A further parallel can be seen with the depiction of the Risen Lord given in the Revelation as the Alpha and Omega, the First and the Last. The fact that these letters were for more than one church parallels with the message of the Revelation, "Let him who has an ear hear what the Spirit says to the churches." Notice that the point is repeatedly made that the message is to be heard by all the churches, not just one specific one. It is a message of all-encompassing importance: Jesus is the author and the finisher of our faith. In the first chapter of Colossians, Paul incorporated "The Christ Hymn" (Colossians 1:14-20), a section of scripture that most scholars assume to be a pre-existing creed that Paul saw as a crystallization of who the church saw Christ to be. Using this pre-existing creed or hymn would not be considered inappropriate or plagiarism any more than if you or I quoted from "Amazing Grace" or the Twenty-third Psalm in one of our speeches or sermons. However, poetry was certainly not outside Paul's abilities.

After all, no one has ever questioned that he penned the magnificent words on love in I Corinthians chapter thirteen. Regardless of whether Paul borrowed an existing hymn or composed his own, this section of the epistle epitomizes the revelation of the Risen Christ.

But the message of the two epistles is not simply a statement about the magnificence of Christ – but an expose on the concluding remark we gleaned from Romans about Christ crushing Satan under our feet and the message that Jesus commanded Paul to preach when He arrested him on the road to Damascus. (Acts 26:18) He says that we are "strengthened with all might, according to his glorious power" (Colossians 1:11) and that the efforts he put forth in the gospel were actually the strivings of God working through him mightily (Colossians 1:29). He recognizes that it is not his or our ability, but the mighty ability of God working through him and us that makes a difference. Verse fifteen of chapter two of Colossians is the climax of the discussion on this powerful authority, "And having spoiled principalities and powers, he made a shew of them openly, triumphing over them in it." The historical context of the imagery used in this passage comes from the ancient practice of humiliating conquered enemies to show that they have been totally subjugated. The term "spoil" means "to strip naked," a reference to the practice of stripping away every vestige of position, authority, honor, and respect from a defeated foe. No longer would the king have his crown, the general his stripes, the athlete his accolades, the soldier his medals, the judge his regalia, the scholar his mortarboard, or the priest his rosary. Now, naked as the day they were born, they would be marched through the streets for all to see that these once feared and respected individuals have nothing to trust in or boast of. Paul furthered this imagery in his second epistle to the Corinthians. In chapter two verse fourteen he said that God always causes us to triumph in

Christ, and in chapter ten verses four and five he spoke of the weapons of our warfare that are mighty through God to pull down strongholds, to cast down imaginations and every high thing that exalts itself against the knowledge of God, and to bring every thought into captivity to the obedience of Christ. The mention of "triumph" is a reference to the above-mentioned practice in which the defeated enemies and all the confiscated treasures were marched through the arch of triumph in celebration of the victory. In this parade, the enemies who were formerly threats are now displayed as slaves with no power or authority. Paul says that God is working in us to bring the enemy of our souls – the devil – to this public display of humiliation in our lives. One interesting observation about the synopsis as recorded in Colossians is that the apostle does not mention the contending with spiritual principalities as he does in Ephesians chapter six. It seems clear that a truly spiritual believer should not have to be taught how to struggle since our real position is one of authority over the forces of the enemy. As Dr. Lester Sumrall used to say, "Flies don't land on hot stoves." Apparently, Paul omitted this emphasis in order to make a clear statement that the struggle is over and that we live in victory over a defeated foe! No wonder the apostle could have maximum impact – he knew that there was nothing capable of stopping him.

Manner of Life

The second element that Paul mentioned as having helped shape Timothy into a man of God was his manner of life. Let's take a little imaginary journey to see if we can gain a bit of insight into this part of the formula that Paul spelled out as his approach to having maximum impact in the lives of those he came in contact with.

"What is going on?" The question kept cycling through his head. "Why is this man talking like this? Doesn't he know that this is almost certainly the last time he'll ever be able to teach us? Doesn't he know that we have all traveled a long way and put out a lot of effort to be here today? Why is he using these few precious minutes to talk about what he has and hasn't done?"

Our friend had been one of the Apostle Paul's followers since the day the preacher showed up on the pleasant Mediterranean shores of Ephesus. Having been a disciple of Apollos who had introduced him to the teachings of John the Baptist, he had eagerly welcomed the evangelist known as a leading spokesman for the new movement that was revitalizing the Jewish faith – that is, when he wasn't stirring up a riot among the Jews who didn't want their faith revitalized. Our friend knew that John the Baptist had told his followers that he was only a messenger to announce the Promised One and that he was expecting to decrease so that the Promised One would be able to increase. Apollos had done an excellent job of showing from the Old Testament how all the prophets had pointed to the same message that John had taught. The only problem was that Apollos didn't know if John had ever revealed who this Promised One was. As far has he knew, King Herod had beheaded the camel-skin-clad preacher before he had been able to identify Him. The day when this new preacher showed up in town made our friend almost giddy with excitement as he wondered if he might be able to help answer some of the questions Apollos had left dangling.

Almost as soon as the new preacher opened his mouth, our friend and his eleven companions realized that he had much to teach them, but it was when he mentioned the Holy Spirit that they realized that not only were they not on the same page with their new teacher – they weren't even in the same textbook. He had patiently taken them through all the basics and brought them "up to speed" on the new faith. Although our friend had been baptized by Apollos in the method that John had taught, he enthusiastically splashed his way into the creek to be baptized in the name of Jesus in acceptance of Paul's teachings. Not only that, he had ecstatically begun to speak with unknown tongues as he came up out of the water – baptized not only in the creek, but also in the Holy Spirit that he had only heard of for the first time that day. From that moment on, our friend felt as if he had been fused to the apostle like a conjoined twin. He was with Paul almost every day over the next three months as he found himself in the local synagogues reasoning with the Jews and then over the next two years as the apostle taught each day in Tyrannus' school building.

What powerful times those were. Every lesson was a new revelation of incredible wisdom as the man who had learned at the feet of the great rabbi Gamaliel and then been taught by the the Lord Himself in the desert of Arabia exposed truth after truth from the Old Testament and showed how they had been fulfilled through the messiah, Jesus of Nazareth. Oh, what wisdom had flowed from his lips every time he opened his mouth. And what powerful miracles followed his words with people being supernaturally healed and set free from demonic control – even without his personally ministering to them, but by simply sending handkerchiefs to them!

His wisdom, authoritative teachings, and miraculous deeds had motivated everyone to such unimaginable heights that they soon were spreading the gospel like an epidemic throughout all Acia Minor until they considered that everyone in the region had heard the message within just two short years. In fact, the gospel had taken such root that some of the local artisans who made their living by selling trinkets at the Temple of Diana actually feared that they would go into bankruptcy due to the dramatic decline in devotees visiting the shrine because they had begun to believe the apostle's message that there is no living god except Jesus. The resulting citywide riot focused on trying to silence this eloquent teacher. The eventual culmination was Paul's miraculous deliverance from a Daniel-versus-the-lions-style encounter.

When Paul eventually left the city, our friend had kept in touch with his mentor through his messengers such as Aquilla, Pricilla, Timothy, and Tychicus; but today, after hearing that the apostle wanted to meet the leaders of the Ephesian church in Miletus as he was traveling to Jerusalem, he had eagerly trekked the forty-six miles for one last visit with his teacher. But no matter how exciting it was to see his master's face again, he was perplexed at the message the apostle had chosen to share. There was nothing of the revelatory insight into the theological mysteries of the gospel, nothing of the stories of the glorious feats of healing or deliverance, no testimonies of the spread of the gospel among the gentiles and Jews alike. Instead, the revered teacher was sharing only about how he had lived among the followers in Ephesus.

> Ye know, from the first day that I came into Asia, after what manner I have been with you at all seasons, Serving the Lord with all humility of mind, and with many tears, and temptations, which befell me by the lying in wait of the Jews: And how I kept back nothing that was profitable unto you, but have shewed you, and have taught you publickly, and from house to house, testifying both to the Jews, and also to the Greeks, repentance toward God, and faith toward our Lord Jesus Christ…Wherefore I take you to record this day, that I am pure

from the blood of all men. For I have not shunned to declare unto you all the counsel of God...Remember, that by the space of three years I ceased not to warn every one night and day with tears...I have coveted no man's silver, or gold, or apparel. Yea, ye yourselves know, that these hands have ministered unto my necessities, and to them that were with me. (Acts 20:18-35)

As Paul was wrapping up his personal ministry to the church, he turned to the one significant factor that genuinely substantiated his work among them – his character. He knew that without integrity, none of his brilliant teachings, supernatural experiences, or mind-boggling exploits would be of any real significance. So in this last visit with the church elders that he loved so much, he wanted to leave them with a validation of his ministry and a directive of how they could similarly confirm their work and lives – integrity of character in motive and action.

Paul knew the principle that lack of character would spoil everything else that might be positive in your life. That is why his last words to these church leaders were to verify his purity of motives and action – and that's why he insisted that Timothy remember what manner of life he had encountered in his mentor.

Purpose

It has been estimated that the Apostle Paul traveled a minimum of ten thousand miles in his quest to fulfill the mission that the Lord had entrusted to him. Remember that this was mostly on foot and usually under adverse circumstances as he was constantly exposed to the elements of nature, the threat of marauders and bandits, and the peril of wild beasts. But he kept pressing forward and was always looking for more and more frontiers to challenge – the mark of a man motivated by purpose. (Acts 19:21, 20:3, 26:16) Yet, there was one particular journey that demonstrated most significantly how this man was motivated by purpose – his final visit to Jerusalem. In Acts chapter twenty-one, we read the story of how Paul was repeatedly warned by individuals within the church that great afflictions awaited him if he continued his journey to Jerusalem. Agabus, the same prophet who predicted the famine that would necessitate the first large-scale benevolence project in the history of the Christian church (Acts 11:28), dramatized the apostle's impending fate by literally tying Paul up with his belt (Acts 21:9-11). With the entire congregation in tears as they pled with him to change his direction, Paul stanchly replied, "What mean ye to weep and to break mine heart? I am ready not to be bound only, but also to die at Jerusalem for the name of the Lord Jesus," a response that left them with only one alternative – to concede, "The will of the Lord be done." However, the prophet's message came as no surprise to Paul since he had already gone on record in his discourse with the leadership from the church at Ephesus who had joined him in Miletus, "I go bound in the spirit unto Jerusalem, not knowing the things that shall befall me there: Save that the Holy Ghost witnesseth in every city, saying that bonds and afflictions abide me. But none of these things move me, neither count I my life dear unto myself, so that I might finish my course with joy, and the ministry, which I have received of the Lord Jesus, to testify the gospel of the grace of God." (Acts 20:22-24) Notice that the apostle's confession was that the Holy Spirit had repeatedly confirmed to him what afflictions he was to face and that he was unmoved by these revelations because he had a greater revelation of the purpose behind the conflicts he was to endure – the opportunity to share the gospel of the grace of God with an unsaved world! This was the very message that Ananias had emphasized when he confronted Paul with his initial decision to become a follower of Christ, "He is a chosen vessel unto me, to bear my name before the Gentiles, and kings, and the children of Israel. I will shew him how great things he must suffer for my name's sake." (Acts 9:15-16) In his communication with the Corinthian believers, Paul made further verification concerning this purposeful commitment, "For our light affliction, which is but for a moment, worketh for us a far more exceeding and eternal weight of glory." (II Corinthians 4:17) Much like the confession of Jesus Christ Himself – for the joy that was set before Him, He endured the cross (Hebrews 12:2) – Paul was no masochist begging for pain; rather he was an optimist rejoicing in the eternal benefit that would result from his commitment to fulfill the purpose behind his temporal sacrifices, challenges, and difficulties.

Faith

Next on Paul's list of determining elements in his ministry to Timothy was his faith – an almost too-big-to-attempt topic. In fact, he uses the word "faith" more than one hundred fifty times in his epistles in addition to a number of references in Acts to his ministry of faith. (Acts 13:8, 14:9, 14:22, 14:27, 16:5, 20:21, 24:24) However, we can find a fairly succinct summarization of Paul's revelation on faith in the tenth chapter of Romans:

> But the righteousness which is of faith speaketh on this wise, Say not in thine heart, Who shall ascend into heaven? (that is, to bring Christ down from above:) Or, Who shall descend into the deep? (that is, to bring up Christ again from the dead.) But what saith it? The word is nigh thee, even in thy mouth, and in thy heart: that is, the

word of faith, which we preach; That if thou shalt confess with thy mouth the Lord Jesus, and shalt believe in thine heart that God hath raised him from the dead, thou shalt be saved. For with the heart man believeth unto righteousness; and with the mouth confession is made unto salvation. For the scripture saith, Whosoever believeth on him shall not be ashamed…So then faith cometh by hearing, and hearing by the word of God. (Romans 10:6-17)

In this passage, we see several significant truths concerning faith that defined Paul's understanding of the subject. First, we see that there is a righteousness – or right standing with God – that is obtained through faith. This relationship with God does not require works – ascending to heaven to find God or descending into the depths of the earth to bring Him back from the grave – to earn His favor. Rather, faith is the release of something that is already inside us. In fact, Paul said in another context that God had already given the necessary faith to every man with the anticipation that each individual would simply activate it. (Romans 12:3) The second thing that Paul addressed in this section on faith is the methodology through which faith is made functional – through the mouth and the heart. Paul clearly defined that there must be two levels of activation for faith to become viable. First, there must be an internal belief in the heart. The concept here is that we must have more than a simple wish, hope, desire, or daydream. There must be a genuine belief inside our hearts that God really does exist and that He is both able and willing to act on our behalf. The companion aspect is that we must verbalize our confession of faith to initiate the desired effect. Contrary to how many may envision faith, Paul insisted that internalization alone without external expression is not genuine faith. Paul would certainly have agreed with the words of his contemporary in the leadership of the early church that internal faith without external works is dead. (James 2:17) One preeminent aspect of Paul's revelation on faith is that it is a product of not only speaking but also hearing – and specifically hearing the truths of the Word of God. Certainly, Paul was referring to the written Word of God that the believers had at that time in the Old Testament, but it is unquestionable that he was also referring to all that God was saying through His Spirit that would eventually become the codified New Testament completion of the Old Testament revelation. Beliefs, hopes, and anticipations based on anything other than what has been specifically spoken by the Lord – either in written scripture or Holy Spirit expression – may be good, motivational, and inspiring; however, they are not genuine faith because faith is the germination of the seed that can only be planted in our hearts by God Himself through His Word and His Spirit.

Longsuffering

In Ephesians 4:2, Paul spoke of the purpose of longsuffering in the church – that of forbearing one another in love. Having already explained in Romans 2:4 and 9:22 that God manifests longsuffering for the purpose of bringing men to salvation, Paul now draws the logical conclusion that longsuffering in the Body of Christ is for the same purpose – to bring our fellow believers to their full salvation. Through patiently working through their errors, immaturity, failures, and even deliberate rebellion, we lovingly hold them in the Body of Christ so that they can develop into strong believers. Paul demonstrated to us that longsuffering is not pampering the errant or enabling them to continue in their failures. His approach – that we would today label as "tough love" – may initially seem radical, but it actually mirrors the approach of our heavenly Father who will allow the prodigal to go to the pigpen yet love him through the whole process. Timothy had a personal opportunity to witness this sort of longsuffering in Paul's dealings with the Corinthian believers. It is amazing how much of his epistles to this congregation is dedicated to the waywardness of the church and the actual hostility that they developed against the apostle in the process. Yet, as Paul addressed and corrected them for their error and attitude, the underlying love that he had for them is evident in his longsuffering acceptance of them as his beloved – howbeit, rebellious – sons (I Corinthians 4:14-15) and the fact that he is perpetually thankful to God for them (I Corinthians 1:4). He point-blankly accused them of being contentious (I Corinthians 1:11), carnal rather than spiritual (I Corinthians 3:1), envious and full of strife (I Corinthians 3:3), and puffed up with pride (I Corinthians 4:18, 5:2). Additionally, he addressed their accusing attitude toward him and the low esteem in which they held him – one whom they could judge (I Corinthians 4:3), a fool while they were full of wisdom (I Corinthians 4:10), defamed, and filthy (I Corinthians 4:13). Paul also recorded their mocking response to his attempts to address their errant ways and attitudes – that he might be bold when writing letters but would cower down in a face-to-face meeting. (I Corinthians 10:1, 10:10-11) Yet, he added that he purposely wanted to spare them any harsh face-to-face confrontation. (I Corinthians 4:19-21, II Corinthians 2:1) and even apologized for disturbing them with his previous letter (II Corinthians 7:8). He went on to describe how that he had even sent his two most trusted assistants to help mediate the conflict (I Corinthians 4:17, II Corinthians (7:7) Yet in all this effort to deal graciously with them, Paul was adamant that he would not renege on his position of their fault (I Corinthians 5:3) and that he would not back down on the necessity for the guilty ones to be dealt with (II Corinthians 13:2).

Timothy also had another personal occasion to witness this principle in operation in Paul's own life in the apostle's dealings with John Mark. Even though Paul refused for John Mark to continue to travel with him after he deserted the team on their initial mission trip (Acts 13:5, 13:13, 15:36-40), Paul later instructed Timothy to bring the restored John Mark to him so that they could spend some time together (II Timothy 4:11).

In Colossians 1:11, Paul added a defining aspect that takes longsuffering to an entirely new level – that of demonstrating longsuffering with joyfulness. It's one thing to put up with other people's problems and shortcomings, but it is an entirely different thing to do so joyfully – without grumbling and accepting the assignment as an unwelcomed burden. Certainly Timothy must have been impacted when he witnessed Paul's forgiving heart toward not only John Mark but all the others who deserted and misused his mentor. (Philippians 1:15-16, II Timothy 4:10, 4:14-16)

Charity

When thinking of charity in connection with the Apostle Paul, our minds immediately race to I Corinthians chapter thirteen, Paul's magnificent expose on love. And I do want to go to that section of scripture at this point – but I want to look at it from a different angle than we might immediate anticipate. The opening verse to this section of scripture is I Corinthians 12:1 in which Paul says, that he would not want the audience to be ignorant concerning spiritual gifts. However, the word "gifts" is actually not in the original Greek text; it was added in by the English translators so that the sentence would not be left hanging by ending with the word "spiritual." Yes, the section of scripture does address gifts, but the addition of "gifts" to the sentence as a viable solution to the awkward translation actually does injustice to the passage. Paul actually addresses much more than just gifts in this section.

> Now there are diversities of gifts, but the same Spirit. And there are differences of administrations, but the same Lord. And there are diversities of operations, but it is the same God which worketh all in all. (I Corinthians 12:4-6)

He speaks of administrations and operations as well as gifts. Therefore, it would be more in order to use a generic word – such as "things" – in the introductory sentence so as to be inclusive of all that Paul wants to communicate here. Notice that each of these categories is associated with a different member of the divine Godhead. The gifts are given by the Holy Spirit as spiritual enduements; the administrations are men and women who possess the spiritual eduements and are positioned by Jesus in the Body of Christ so that they can minister in their giftings; the operations are the godly attitudes given by the Father through which the ministers function as they display their spiritual enduements. This is the triple trinity: the trinity of God, the trinity of gifts, administrations, and operations, and the trinity of enduements, ministers, and motivations. Paul specifically listed the spiritual gifts in verses eight through ten: the word of wisdom, the word or knowledge, faith, gifts of healing, working of miracles, discerning spirits, diverse kinds of tongues, and the interpretation of tongues. He enumerated at least a partial list of the administrations of the Lord in verses twenty-eight through thirty: apostles, prophets, teachers, miracles, gifts of healing, helps, governments, and those who speak in diversities of tongues. He then defined the operations of God in the thirteenth verse of chapter thirteen: faith, hope, and love.

Even though the focus of the thirteenth chapter is on love, the implication is that nothing that we do in ministry is profitable unless it is motivated by the heart attitude of the heavenly Father – including faith and hope as well as love. Paul emphasized that any heroic act – even martyrdom – and all our charitable works – like giving every penny we have to feed the poor or house the homeless – would be totally pointless unless they are motivated by the Father's nature. (I Corinthians 13:3) Without question, Timothy had seen these heroic acts and charitable works in Paul's life, but Paul wanted to emphasize that it was not the actions themselves that his protégé was to focus on – it was the motivation behind them that mattered. Additionally, Paul stressed that all the supernatural miracles that manifest in our lives through the gifts of the Holy Spirit are pointless without the Father's heart motivation. He specifically used the illustrations of a sounding brass and a tinkling cymbal when referring to speaking in tongues without the proper operation of the godly nature. (I Corinthians 13:1) This allusion helps clarify a couple verses in the previous chapter that would otherwise seem to be spurious or out of place.

> Ye know that ye were Gentiles, carried away unto these dumb idols, even as ye were led. Wherefore I give you to understand, that no man speaking by the Spirit of God calleth Jesus accursed: and that no man can say that Jesus is the Lord, but by the Holy Ghost. (I Corinthians 12:2-3)

The reference to idolatry is directly linked to the cymbal and brass in that pagan temples incorporate these instruments to invoke demonic presence when devotees come to worship. Above the entranceways in all Hindu temples hang little bells that the worshipers ring as they cross the threshold. The tinkle of those bells is supposed to awaken the spirits that abide in the temple. Buddhist shrines have gongs that are sounded at the beginning of their ceremonies – again to awaken the demons associated with the shrine. Timothy had witnessed some incredible miracles in the public ministry of his mentor and had undoubtedly seen even more manifestations of the supernatural in Paul's private life; yet, the apostle wanted to remind his disciple that it was the charity – not the miracles – that made him who he was and allowed him to have maximum impact.

Patience

Although we often think of longsuffering and patience as being essentially synonymous, Paul obviously saw them as distinctly different qualities that demanded being listed separately as he addressed the qualities in his life that had impacted the life of his disciple. In looking at longsuffering, we saw that the apostle saw this quality mainly in relationship to our ministry to others; however, it seems that he was more focused on the development of the individual believer when he spoke of patience. Notice how he attributed patience as a major role in the development of a godly character in Romans 5:3-5, "And not only so, but we glory in tribulations also: knowing that tribulation worketh patience; And patience, experience; and experience, hope: And hope maketh not ashamed; because the love of God is shed abroad in our hearts by the Holy Ghost which is given unto us." Interestingly enough, Paul also equated patience with miracles as a characteristic that qualified him for apostleship, "Truly the signs of an apostle were wrought among you in all patience, in signs, and wonders, and mighty deeds." (II Corinthians 12:12) In essence, patience is that quality that allows us to let God have the time to work in us and bring us to the place that His character and power can flow through us. Although there is no specific mention of Timothy in the account of Paul's encounter with the damsel in Philippi who was possessed with a spirit of divination (Acts 16:16-18), it is likely that he was with the apostle during this time since it seems that he had accompanied Paul from Lystra (Acts 16:3) and stayed with him until Paul left him behind in Berea (Acts 17:14). If this is the case, the disciple witnessed an excellent example of his mentor's life of patience. The narrative makes it very clear that the demoniac followed Paul and his companions for many days crying out that they were servants of the most high God. It is also clear that this practice grieved the apostle. We are not given any details concerning this encounter – perhaps she was mocking them with the tone of voice she used to make the proclamation, perhaps she was using terminology that suggested that they were actually messengers of some pagan god rather than the true and living God, or perhaps it was just simply that the apostle couldn't stand the fact that his publicity agent was the devil. Regardless of the circumstances behind the event, the one thing that we know is that the apostle put up with this annoyance for many days even though the whole event was tremendously disturbing to him – patience! When God had done all that needed to be done in the heart and life of the apostle through this difficult experience, Paul turned to the girl and through the authority birthed out of his patience – with one simple sentence – set the girl free and totally changed her whole life!

Persecutions

You could read his body like a book. It was a journal that chronicled his life. His back was a veritable roadmap connecting almost every major city in Israel, Turkey, Greece, and Italy with scars from beatings he had received in each place. Five different lashings of thirty-nine stripes each had left potholes from the violence of the whips as they literally snatched chunks of tissue from his torso. Ribbons of scar tissue testified to the lesions caused as the whips tore through his flesh. The hesitancy in his gait was witness of the three times he had been clubbed. The bald patches on his chest where the skin had been rubbed so raw that no chest hair would grow were the mementoes of the three different times he had spent whole days and nights desperately clinging to pieces of driftwood to keep from drowning after having been shipwrecked in the Mediterranean. Jagged claw marks on his forearms and the scar that ran dangerously close to his jugular vein were evidences of his struggle with wild beasts in Ephesus. The calluses around his wrists and ankles were the signatures left by the chains and shackles from almost every prison between Jerusalem and Rome.   The two companion puncture wounds on the inside of his arm were a souvenir left behind by a venomous serpent on the island of Melita. The contusions on the side of his face were reminders of the day he was stoned and left for dead in Lystra. Yet, as he ran his left hand across this ledger of injuries, he picked up a pen and parchment in his right hand and scratched out the memorable words, "Our light affliction, which is but for a moment, worketh for us a far more exceeding and eternal weight of glory." (II Corinthians 4:17) How could it be? Why would the Apostle Paul say such a thing? Simply because he was convinced that no amount of persecution could separate him from the love of God in Christ Jesus, "Who shall separate us from the love of Christ? shall tribulation, or distress, or persecution, or famine, or nakedness, or peril, or sword?" (Romans 8:35)   With this kind of revelation concerning his condition, Paul was in an unshakable position that he described in Romans 12:12, "Rejoicing in hope; patient in tribulation; continuing constant in prayer." He summarized the topic when writing to his disciple Timothy with one overwhelming warning accompanied with an even more overwhelming promise.

Yea, and all that will live godly in Christ Jesus shall suffer persecution. But evil men and seducers shall wax worse and worse, deceiving and being deceived. But continue thou in the things which thou hast learned and hast been assured of, knowing of whom thou hast earned them; and that from a child thou hast known the holy scriptures, which are able to make thee wise unto salvation through faith which is in Christ Jesus. All scripture is given by inspiration of God, and is profitable for doctrine, for reproof, for correction, for instruction in righteousness; that the man of God may be perfect, thoroughly furnished unto all good works. (I Timothy 3:12-17)

It was this confidence in the fact that God is being glorified through his suffering that motivated Paul to bear the attacks of the religious crowds and hostile governments without retaliation, grumbing, feeling sorry for himself, or even attempting to avoid these attacks. In fact, he truly gloried in the privilege of bearing the marks of Christ in his own body. (Romans 8:18; II Corinthians 1:5-7, 2:4, 4:16, 6:4, 8:2; Galatians 3:17, 5:11, 6:12; Ephesians 3:1, 4:1, 6:20; Philippians 1:7, 1:13-16, 1:29, 3:8, 3:10, 4:12, 4:14; Colossians 1:24, 4:3, 4:18; I Thessalonians 2:2, 3:4, 3:7; II Thessalonians 1:5; I Timothy 4:10; II Timothy 1:8, 1:12, 2:9) It is also through this same confidence that he encouraged Timothy to boldly and bravely accept the persecution that would be targeted toward him. (II Timothy 1:8, 2:3, 2:12, 3:12, 4:2)

In the passage under consideration today, Paul specifically directed Timothy's attention to the suffering that he endured in Antioch, Iconium, and Lystra. Although we have no biblical proof of the connection between these events and his disciple Timothy, we should remember that Paul and Timothy first connected in Lystra. (Acts 16:1) Although this connection was some time after the events spoken of here (Acts 13:14-14:23), there is every possibility that young Timothy would have heard about – or even been an eyewitness to – these momentous events that occurred in "his own backyard." If so, it is not unlikely that such prior knowledge of the man who was chased out of town, harassed, stoned to death, and raised back to life – and yet kept on with his mission – was the testimony that motivated Timothy to willingly submit himself to circumcision and abandon all to become the man's disciple. If there is reality to this proposed scenario, then we can see why the apostle could take glory in his sufferings – he knew that there was good that would come out of them. His blood did become seed in the life of Timothy – and countless others.

The Church at Thessalonica

Out of all the congregations that felt the impact of Paul's life, I'd like for us to consider one specific church as an example of maximum impact because this particular congregation was birthed out of just three weeks of the apostle's ministry – yet it became a viable and enduring church that, according to Paul's own evaluation, was an example to all the believers in Macedonia and Achaia and the epicenter from which the gospel was sounded throughout Macedonia and Achaia and beyond. (I Thessalonians 1:7-8) In spite of the fact – or possibly enhanced by the fact – that this church was birthed in much persecution by opponents who were not satisfied to just wreak havoc locally but actually followed Paul to his next destination to engender even more violence (Acts 17:5-9,

17:13), the congregation stood strong and flourished. Yet Paul was able to define in one concise passage what he did in Thessalonica that left such a powerful impact, "For our gospel came not unto you in word only, but also in power, and in the Holy Ghost, and in much assurance; as ye know what manner of men we were among you for your sake." (I Thessalonians 1:5)

The Word

The first avenue he mentioned was the Word. In fact, Paul's writings are full of instruction to avoid various substitutes that can camouflage themselves as worthy ministry material but actually lead to confusion and disqualification of our ministries: philosophy (Colossians 2:8), vain deceit (Colossians 2:8), the tradition of men (Colossians 2:8), the rudiments of the world (Colossians 2:8), enticing words of man's wisdom (I Corinthians 2:4), profane and vain babblings (I Timothy 6:20, II Timothy 2:16), oppositions of science falsely so called (I Timothy 6:20), fables (I Timothy 1:4, II Timothy 4:4), Jewish fables (Titus 1:14), profane and old wives' fables (I Timothy 4:7), endless genealogies (I Timothy 1:4, Titus 3:9), the commandments of men (Titus 1:14), foolish and unlearned questions (II Timothy 2:23, Titus 3:9), teachers having itching ears (II Timothy 4:3), teaching things which they ought not for filthy lucre's sake (Titus 1:11), strivings about the law (Titus 3:9), the doctrines of men (Colossians 2:22), and even doctrines of devils (I Timothy 4:1). Paul himself had a personal experience with the temptation to make a substitute. Remember the sermon he preached to the philosophers on Mars Hill in Athens.

> Ye men of Athens, I perceive that in all things ye are too superstitious. For as I passed by, and beheld your devotions, I

found an altar with this inscription, To The Unknown God. Whom therefore ye ignorantly worship, him declare I unto you. God that made the world and all things therein, seeing that he is Lord of heaven and earth, dwelleth not in temples made with hands; Neither is worshipped with men's hands, as though he needed any thing, seeing he giveth to all life, and breath, and all things; And hath made of one blood all nations of men for to dwell on all the face of the earth, and hath determined the times before appointed, and the bounds of their habitation; That they should seek the Lord, if haply they might feel after him, and find him, though he be not far from every one of us: For in him we live, and move, and have our being; as certain also of your own poets have said, For we are also his offspring. Forasmuch then as we are the offspring of God, we ought not to think that the Godhead is like unto gold, or silver, or stone, graven by art and man's device. And the times of this ignorance God winked at; but now commandeth all men every where to repent: Because he hath appointed a day, in the which he will judge the world in righteousness by that man whom he hath ordained; whereof he hath given assurance unto all men, in that he hath raised him from the dead. (Acts 17:22-31)

Notice the obvious lack of the name of Jesus in this message – the name that Paul elsewhere described as the name above all others (Philippians 2:9-11) and the one through which men can be saved (Romans 10:13). There is also an absence of any reference to Paul's own personal testimony – the standard fare in much of his preaching. Additionally, he quoted their secular poets rather than making any reference to the Old Testament prophets – a common element in his other presentations of the gospel. The end result was that he left behind no viable church in the city – unlike his ministry in almost every other place he visited. Have you ever noticed that Paul visited Ephesus, left behind a church and wrote a letter to them and that he did the same in Galatia, in Philippi, in Thessalonica, in Corinth, and in Colossi – but that there is no letter to the church in Athens because one did not exist? Paul obviously realized the ineffectiveness of this "seeker sensitive" approach in that he totally changed his approach when moving to the next city on his journey – Corinth.

> I, brethren, when I came to you, came not with excellency of speech or of wisdom, declaring unto you the testimony of God.
> For I determined not to know any thing among you, save Jesus Christ, and him crucified. (I Corinthians 2:1-2)

Power

Paul's second avenue was power. In a passage we have already mentioned, the apostle described what made his Jerusalem-to-Illyricum ministry effective: mighty signs and wonders, by the power of the Spirit of God. (Romans 15:19) All we need is a quick review of his ministry to see that it was, indeed, accompanied with miraculous events. (Acts 13:11, 16:16-18, 19:11, 20:9-10, 28:3-6) However, we may be tempted to relegate such supernatural occurrences to ancient history or to the lives of such men of stature as this apostle of the faith. The truth is that this same supernatural assistance is available for – and actually expected to be operative in – the ministry of all believers

(Mark 16:17-18). Some people may respond to – and even recoil at – the concept of the necessity of the demonstration of supernatural power in the ministering of our gifts by questioning why it would be considered necessary to display such supernatural power in any and every ministry. They might feel that such displays of divine power should be reserved for evangelists and crusaders. In a sense, such a conclusion is at least partially true. Paul did teach that these supernatural manifestations are given to different members of the Body of Christ as they would have special need of their operation (I Corinthians 12:11); however, in the same section of scripture he emphasized that each person should have some form of supernatural operation in his ministry (I Corinthians 12:7). Although every person may not require the ministry of healing in order to adequately serve in his gifting, he will need at least one of God's supernatural forms of empowerment in this endeavor. For example, even in the compassion ministry of feeding the hungry and clothing the naked we will need the gift of faith that is listed right alongside the gift of healing. (I Corinthians 12:7) Without the supernatural manifestation of faith, no one will ever be able to finance the gargantuan challenge. In addition, we all need the supernatural assistance afforded us through speaking in tongues that Paul described as an avenue of personal edification (I Corinthians 14:4) – a personal strengthening which is absolutely necessary to meet the challenges of any ministry.

The Holy Spirit

Next, Paul mentioned the Holy Ghost. In that the operation of the gifts seems to have been his topic in the previous category, we must interpret this reference to suggest a fuller meaning of the operation of the Holy Spirit in the believer's life. Turning to his letter to the Galatians, we see at least two areas where the Holy Spirit's influence must be evidenced in a believer's life and ministry. The first is in chapter five verses sixteen and eighteen: walking in and being led by the Spirit. Such Holy Spirit orchestrated movement is not only vitally important to the success of our personal lives and the productivity of our ministries; it may also make the difference between life and death. As Paul mentioned in the Galatian passage, the fatally destructive works of the flesh will overcome us unless we walk in the Spirit. In addition to the example we have already examined in how the apostle was directed away from Asia toward a fertile ministry in Europe through the Holy Spirit's direction, it would be good to remember how the inner voice of the Holy Spirit warned Paul of the impending danger into which his ship was to sail. (Acts 27:10) The other Holy Spirit quality that Paul discusses in Galatians chapter five is the fruit of the Spirit listed in verses twenty-two and twenty-three. Just as no one cares for a barren tree that does not produce fruit, people will not be attracted to our lives or ministries unless we manifest the fruit of the Spirit.

Much Assurance

Paul followed with the quality of assurance. Even without an examination of some of the key biblical injunctions concerning assurance (Isaiah 32:17, Acts 17:31, Colossians 2:2, Hebrews 6:11, 10:22), we can recognize from the natural world that we never want to believe what someone is saying if we don't feel that he really believes it himself. Paul was persuaded of the validity of his message (Romans 8:38, 14:14, II Timothy 1:12) and admonished his disciples to be fully persuaded concerning their faith (Romans 14:5).

Allow me interject a little personal story at this point. A dear friend of mine in California was diagnosed as having an advanced case of the most aggressive strain of cancer. Her doctor was so concerned because of the rapid growth of this malignancy that he advised her to leave his office and go directly to the airport and book the first flight available to a certain clinic in Texas that was the only facility able to treat this form of cancer. He told her that the time she would waste going home to pack a suitcase would be critical considering the aggressive nature of her malady. The doctor was totally certain that his diagnosis was correct because he had had it confirmed by ninety doctors who worked under him at a major medical facility. Outside the doctor's office, my friend's husband asked if she wanted to go directly to the airport as she had been advised. Her response was that she first wanted to go to the church in accordance with James 5:14-15, "Is any sick among you? let him call for the elders of the church; and let them pray over him, anointing him with oil in the name of the Lord: And the prayer of faith shall save the sick, and the Lord shall raise him up." Their pastor called all the elders of the church together for a special prayer meeting and laid hands on my friend; however, she could sense doubt behind their prayer "of faith." One of them made the comment that when we get to heaven we will all be totally healed and have perfect bodies. That, of course, was a true report; but it was not a good report (Philippians 4:8) for a woman who was asking God to heal her while she was still here on earth! After leaving the church office, she told her husband that she could hear what they were saying with their lips but could also read what they were thinking by looking at their eyes, faces, and body language – and the two did not agree. She told him, "These people are not going to heal me; they are going to kill me! Please get me to a place where people really believe what they say!" When he promised to take her anywhere an airplane could fly, she asked to go to Indiana to be with my wife and me. They flew out on the next flight, and I arranged for special prayer by two great apostles – our pastor, Dr. Lester Sumrall, and the pastor of the world's largest congregation, Dr. Yonggi Cho. She then spent the next three days in our home and received a constant diet of faith-filled words that came with confidence out of our hearts, not just words out of our heads. My wife and I did nothing but reinforce the promises of God's Word concerning healing. When our friend did eventually make it to the clinic, the doctor refused to admit her because he couldn't find even a trace of cancer in her body! Assurance made a life-and-death difference in her case. Remember that her doctor told her that she didn't even have time to pack a suitcase? Well, that was over twenty-five years ago. Imagine how may suitcases she has packed in that quarter of a century!

The Manner of Man I Was Among You for Your Sake

Character was the fifth avenue through which Paul conveyed his gift. In this passage, he speaks of the manner of man he was among them for their sakes – not for his own sake, but for their sake. Here we see a different focus from his reference to character as one of the characteristics that influenced Timothy's life. In this context Paul was saying that he lived a good, moral life not so that he could guarantee <u>his</u> salvation but so that he could ensure <u>their</u> salvation. In I Corinthians 10:27-33, Paul made the point that our actions must be weighted – not by our own consciences – but by the consciences of those who see our actions. He understood that even though all things were technically lawful for him, it was not in his best interest to always use his liberty because that freedom might cause a brother to stumble in his faith. (I Corinthians 6:12, Romans 14:21) One contemporary pastor aptly paraphrased what Paul was trying to say, "It's a lot easier for me to get myself to heaven than it is for me to get you there." Another pastor illustrated the necessity of living a life of character by saying, "People read the gospels of Matthew, Mark, Luke, and John and the epistles of Timothy, Peter, James, and Paul," while pointing toward individuals in the audience with those names. He then went on to confirm the point by adding, "Now you know why your mamma named you like she did!"

In the second chapter of I Thessalonians, Paul actually goes to some lengths to explain what he meant by the reference to the life that he lived before the Thessalonians. Notice that he concluded this lengthy expose with the deduction that it was because of the way he presented himself before these new believers that they received the gospel as the very Word of God rather than just the words of a mere man – proof positive that our lives really do become the gospel that the people read and believe!

> For yourselves, brethren, know our entrance in unto you, that it was not in vain: But even after that we had suffered before, and were shamefully entreated, as ye know, at Philippi, we were bold in our God to speak unto you the gospel of God with much contention. For our exhortation was not of deceit, nor of uncleanness, nor in guile: But as we were allowed of God to be put in trust with the gospel, even so we speak; not as pleasing men, but God, which trieth our hearts. For neither at any time used we flattering words, as ye know, nor a cloke of covetousness; God is witness: Nor of men sought we glory, neither of you, nor yet of others, when we might have been burdensome, as the apostles of Christ. But we were gentle among you, even as a nurse cherisheth her children: So being affectionately desirous of you, we were willing to have imparted unto you, not the gospel of God only, but also our own souls,

because ye were dear unto us. For ye remember, brethren, our labour and travail: for labouring night and day, because we would not be chargeable unto any of you, we preached unto you the gospel of God. Ye are witnesses, and God also, how holily and justly and unblameably we behaved ourselves among you that believe: As ye know how we exhorted and comforted and charged every one of you, as a father doth his children, That ye would walk worthy of God, who hath called you unto his kingdom and glory. For this cause also thank we God without ceasing, because, when ye received the word of God which ye heard of us, ye received it not as the word of men, but as it is in truth, the word of God, which effectually worketh also in you that believe. (I Thessalonian 2:1-13)

Paul's Own Confession about Himself

Up to this point, our study has focused mainly on what the Apostle Paul did and how he was able to accomplish such significant things; however, the real key to why he was able to make such an impact is who he was. Although Paul was one of the most prolific writers and most eloquent spokesmen of the New Testament era, we can single out a handful of his statements that clearly define how he saw himself and the ministry to which he was called.

Servant of God

We first met Paul at the stoning of Stephen, the first Christian martyr. In this introductory encounter, we saw that he was an activist and that he was dedicated to serving his cause. Even though the story leaves us with the impression that Saul never actually hurled any stones at poor Steven, he took an active role in the execution through encouraging the ones who actually took the martyr's life. He did, however, follow up after this episode by gaining permission from the high priest to further the persecution of the infant church. Acts 9:1 describes him as breathing out threatenings and slaughter against the disciples – picture a bull in the bullring in Barcelona! The hostility that we see displayed in his actions might lead us to wonder exactly what kind of person this man was. Was he a criminal or a mobster of some sort? No! He was actually a noble citizen – an orthodox Jew of culture and religious pedigree. In his own words, we can see that he was a most proper Jew.

> Though I might also have confidence in the flesh. If any other man thinketh that he hath whereof he might trust in the flesh, I more: Circumcised the eighth day, of the stock of Israel, of the tribe of Benjamin, an Hebrew of the Hebrews; as touching the law, a

Pharisee; Concerning zeal, persecuting the church; touching the righteousness which is in the law, blameless. (Philippians 3:4-6)

Since Paul was not a typical street ruffian, why did he do such horrible things against Stephen and other Christians prior to his conversion? Perhaps we can find the answer in the words of Jesus, "They that kill you think they do God service." (John 16:2) Saul was a man of service, and he zealously served God (or so he thought) by trying to wipe out the new heresy – Christianity. Yet, at the height of this career of what he thought was a service to the Lord, something radical happened that made him discount all accomplishments and the credentials he had gained to this point. (Philippians 3:7) On the road to Damascus, he was apprehended – put under arrest – by the Lord. (Philippians 3:12) Ironically, he was arrested as he was arresting others. With this arrest, he was conscripted as a true servant of the Lord. (Acts 27:23; Romans 1:1, 1:9; Galatians 1:10; II Timothy 1:3; Titus 1:1) As His servant, God used this apostle to author a dozen of the New Testament books – some of the greatest literature ever written. The Apostle Paul traveled at his own expense through the then-known world to preach and teach in every city where he could find an opening. (Acts 18:3, 28:30; I Corinthians 9:12) Additionally, he went through strenuous Jewish rituals to pacify the Jewish brethren and endured unimaginable hardships to further the cause (Acts 21:22-27, II Corinthians 11:23-33), but he adamantly proclaimed that he did not consider it a burden to give himself away like this (I Corinthians 9.19-23). In fact, to the very end of his life, he was continually hoping for more opportunities to serve God. This life of total sacrifice was in Paul's mind simply his "reasonable service." (Romans 12:1) He knew that life not in service to God would be a life in service to some other master.

Know ye not, that to whom ye yield yourselves servants to obey, his servants ye are to whom ye obey; whether of sin unto death, or of obedience unto righteousness? But God be thanked, that ye were the servants of sin, but ye have obeyed from the heart that form of doctrine which was delivered you. Being then made free from sin, ye became the servants of righteousness. (Romans 6:16-18)

Man of Destiny

In Galatians 1:15, Paul said that God had separated him from his mother's womb – suggesting that his life – like those of Isaiah (Isaiah 49:1), Jeremiah (Jeremiah 1:5), and David (Psalm 22:9) – was destined even before his birth. In fact, Paul even suggested that his destiny was preconceived even before Creation. (Ephesians 1:4) Even though Paul was officially ordained by the elders in Antioch (Acts 13:2), he repeatedly insisted that he was made an apostle by God, not by men (Romans 1:1, I Corinthians 1:1, II Corinthians 1:1,Galatians 1:1, Ephesians 1:1, Colossians 1:1, I Timothy 1:1, II Timothy 1:1) – a testimony to the fact that he saw his position in life as nothing less than a divine destiny. In I Corinthians 15:8, Paul described his encounter with Jesus on the road to Damascus as "of one born out of due time." For centuries, theologians have debated the exact meaning of this unusual phrase, with some saying that it is a reference to the appearance of Jesus as if He were a premature baby and others insisting that the reference is to the fact that Paul encountered Him in an unlikely chronological timeframe – after His death and resurrection rather than during His physical lifetime. Since Jesus' appearance to Saul was as a brilliant light, the first argument of the premature baby seems totally unsubstantiated.

However, the idea that Paul is making reference to an unusual chronology seems to fit well since the two men were likely in Jerusalem at the same time but it seems that their paths never crossed. If we adopt the approach that the reference is to the timeframe of the encounter rather than to the appearance of Christ, there could be a connection to a statement from the testimony that Paul made when he presented his case before King Agrippa. In recounting the words that Jesus spoke to him on the road to Damascus, Paul said that Jesus had called him to be a witness of the things he had seen. (Acts 26:16) Notice that Jesus spoke of <u>things</u> – plural – that Paul had seen. This is obviously a reference to more than just the encounter on the Damascus road since that would have been one singular <u>thing</u>. So what were the other things? We know from Romans 16:7 that Paul had relatives (Andronicus and Junia) who were believers before his encounter with Christ. It is likely that they would have shared their faith with him and that he rejected their witness. Further, there is a possibility that Paul had had some mitigating influence from his master Gamaliel, who even though he was a member of the Sanhedrin had a surprising openness to the possibility that the Christian movement might genuinely be of God. (Acts 5:34-39) Perhaps Gamaliel had shared his feelings with his student who refused to listen. If this were the case, there is no question that he would later look back on the day when he refused the temperance of his teacher and declared that he had miscarried or even aborted the opportunity to open his heart to the new faith so many days, months, or even years earlier. Of course, standing in the crowd listening to Stephen's impassioned speech and witnessing his confession of faith as he became the first Christian martyr would have certainly been an excellent opportunity for Saul to have "seen the light," but instead he held the coats of those who threw the stones that paved the path for Stephen to make his way to Jesus and the Father. (Acts 6:8-7:60) If these encounters were the "things" that Jesus spoke of, then it is evident that Paul's faith journey didn't begin on the road to Damascus; rather, destiny was already at work when he held the coats for the lynch mob who took the life of the first Christian martyr, when he made the decision to study religion at the feet of Gamaliel, and more dramatically in Paul's "prehistory" in his mother's womb and even before. To Paul, being born out of time meant that even though he wasn't born again until his adulthood, God was actually trying to make him into a minister from – and even before – his very birth. This was destiny at work, making Paul into a man who could deliver maximum impact.

Knowing that there is a destiny for one's life gives a totally new perspective to each day and every event. For example, Paul could declare that none of the treats that awaited him in Jerusalem moved him because he knew that there was a destiny beyond whatever his opponents could do to him. (Acts 20:24) Jesus testified that he knew that there was an appointed time for His destiny; therefore, nothing that the enemy could attempt against Him prior to that time would be successful. (John 2:4, 7:6, 7:8, 7:30, 8:20) He also knew that He was ready to fulfill His destiny when the appointed time came. (Matthew 18:21; John 13:1, 17:1) I have actually seen the impact of destiny in my own life in that my conception and birth were the direct answer to a covenant prayer that my mother prayed. Believing for many years that she should have another child, she eventually resorted to the prayer of Hannah from I Samuel 1:11, "Give unto thine handmaid a man child, then I will give him unto the Lord all the days of his life." When she became pregnant with me the following month, she knew that there was to be a special destiny upon my life – a destiny that even death could not deter.

My first close encounter with the Grim Reaper was when I was still a baby in my mother's arms. Of course, all I know about that is what my mother has told me. It seems that we were driving through the cemetery – an ideal place to face the harbinger of death. But the story is not quite macabre as it may sound – I think that my parents were visiting the gravesite of a recently departed friend. Well, anyway, the story goes that I reached up and grabbed the door handle. These were the days before baby seats and seat belts; so, I was sitting in my mother's lap. When the door swung open, I went with it and tumbled out of the car, landing underneath the moving vehicle. Thank the Lord, we were in that cemetery. Had we been on a public street, my father would have been going faster than the ten miles an hour he was driving as we toured the grounds. When the car came to a stop, my mother leapt out to find me in the direct path of the oncoming back tire. I was only an inch from certain death. Over the years, I've often pondered that story and have come to realize that it is inseparably linked with another episode that my mother has related to me – the one about God's divine purpose for my life

Facing the Grim Reaper and winning can give you a new perspective on life. Coming back the victor from an encounter with our final enemy can produce a boldness and confidence in God that propels us toward unlimited adventures in living. It was in the beautiful Sierra Mountains of California that I had my most dramatic confrontation with certain death. I suppose that there must be something prophetic about the very name of the place: the Devil's Slide and the Angel's Falls. As a cool mountain stream rushes across the polished granite surface of the mountain, it produces an exhilarating natural waterslide that would be the envy of any water park. So steep and so wild, it couldn't be called anything short of the Devil's Slide. Abruptly, it comes to the spectacular point where the water rushes into

96

thin air and plummets over the Angel's Falls into a crystal pool below. Well, I'm the sort of person can't pass up a chance to try an adventure like this. However, I stepped on a slick rock at the top of the slide and I lost my footing. I began sliding down the polished granite mountain – but not on the waterslide. Instead, I was headed for a precipice that would toss me over a several-hundred-foot cliff to certain death on the rocks below. I could hear the other people on the mountain screaming, "He's going to die!" as I tumbled closer and closer to death's door. All along, I knew that safety was only a few feet away if I could only get away from the cliff. Throwing my weight to the left, I managed to change my course of fall by the matter of inches it took to direct myself away from the cliff and toward the pool at the bottom of Angel's Falls. That pool was my only hope. At the last possible second, I tumbled over a ledge and into the pool. Well, not exactly into the pool – I was traveling so fast at that point, that I actually overshot the pool and slammed into the rock wall on the other side. I'm certain that I must have looked like the cartoon character Wile E. Coyote when, in his chase of the Roadrunner, he flattens himself against the canyon wall and then peels off like wallpaper having lost its adhesive. After splashing into the water once I smacked against the stone face, I came up for a breath to hear the strangers at the top of Devil's Slide rejoice, "He's alive!" I was alive and to prove it I climbed out of the pool and headed to the top of the mountain for a trip down the Devil's Slide. As I stepped into the chilly stream, an astonished onlooker asked, "Aren't you the guy that was almost killed?" To an outsider, it seemed strange that I would even want to go down that mountain side again – but having faced death and won, I knew what the Holy Spirit meant when He directed the author of Hebrews to pen the words: "destroy him that had the power of death, that is, the devil; and deliver them who through fear of death were all their lifetime subject to bondage." (Hebrews 2: 14-15) There is bondage in the fear of death; yet, as believers, we can destroy the power of the devil because we know the One who is the Resurrection and Life. Because Jesus is Life itself, He determines the fate of those whom He has marked with destiny. And, truly, every one of us has a God-given purpose that He determined even before He created the world – including the Devil's Slide and Angel Falls! (Ephesians 1:4)

Heavenly Vision

In his testimony before king Agrippa, Paul spoke of the "heavenly vision" that changed his life on the road to Damascus. (Acts 26:19) It has been said that a missionary is not made by crossing the sea but by seeing the cross – and in Paul's life, it is true that the vision of Jesus on the road to Damascus is what gave him a mission, "But rise, and stand upon thy feet: for <u>I have appeared unto thee for this purpose, to make thee a minister and a witness</u> both of these things which thou hast seen, and of those things in the which I will appear unto thee; Delivering thee from the people, and from the Gentiles, unto whom now I send thee, <u>To open their eyes, and to turn them from darkness to light</u>, and from the power of Satan unto God, that they may receive forgiveness of sins, and inheritance among them which are sanctified by faith that is in me." (Acts 26:16-18) It is amazing that the Lord spoke to a man who was blinded by the light of Jesus that his mission would be open the eyes of the blind so that they could see that same light of the gospel.

But what did that encounter birth inside of Paul that made him the missionary that he became? In his letter to the Romans Paul made three simple, yet profound, confessions that summarize the results of what happened in him when he saw the cross and was transformed from Saul of Tarsus into Paul the apostle – a man who made maximum impact.

Debtor

In chapter one verse fourteen of Romans, he declared, "I am debtor both to the Greeks, and to the Barbarians; both to the wise, and to the unwise." His mission was one of obligation. It was impossible for him to remain silent in any situation because of the impact of that encounter with Jesus. Of course, we know that he was already a very zealous individual. By his own confession, he outdid everyone in his persecution of the church and in his keeping of the Jewish traditions and even considered himself totally blameless in terms of the impossible feat of keeping the total Law. (Galatians 1:13-14, Philippians 3:6) Yet the fervor of his previous life paled in comparison to the dynamic thrust of this new mission in which the apostle felt an obligation to preach this gospel to every individual everywhere. To Paul, the ministry was not a job. In fact, he explained to the Corinthians that even though he had every legitimate right to receive a salary from them, he had determined to cover his own expenses so that no one would ever misinterpret his motivation. (I Corinthians 4:12, 9:1-23) When he called the elders of the church at Ephesus to Miletus for his farewell message, he asked them to reaffirm that his ministry had been without any desire for personal gain. (Acts 20:33-34) We get the modern concept of self-supporting "tentmaking" ministries from Paul's practice working at a secular job. (Acts 18:3) But this is not the extent of his commitment – he not only cared for his own needs, but he also expended his own monetary resources and physical and emotional strength to minister the gospel. (II Corinthians 12:15) To Paul, the ministry was not a position, promotion, or power. In the farewell speech to the Ephesian elders, Paul accentuated, "Ye know, from the first day that I came into Asia, after what manner I have been with you at all seasons, Serving the Lord with all humility of mind, and with many tears, and temptations, which befell me by the lying in wait of the Jews: And how I kept back nothing that was profitable unto you, but have shewed you, and have taught you publicly, and from house to house" (Acts 20:18-20) – stressing the fact that he did nothing to promote his own position or even to accept a position that others might want to elevate him to. His mission was not about personal gain or advancement – but about establishing others in the kingdom.   In fact, he even described his ministry as becoming poor to make others rich. (II Corinthians 6:10)

Ready

Paul's second declaration that defined his mission is in the following verse, "So, as much as in me is, I am ready to preach the gospel to you that are at Rome also." (Romans 1:15) Seeing the cross not only made him a debtor, it also made him ready to preach the gospel. Other than the self-imposed exile into Arabia to sort out the meaning of this new experience, there is not even the slightest hint that Paul ever took a vacation, a day off, or a leave of absence from his mission. From the moment he received his revelation, Saul was destined to be given the platform to stand on – even before kings – to expound that revelation. (Acts 9:15, 26:16-18) The fact that he may not have had the most coveted conditions under which to minister this revelation to these men did not hamper the effectiveness with which he delivered his gift to them. (Acts 13:12, 26:28)   His assessment of his ministry as covering the territory from Jerusalem to Illyricum confirms the principle that his gifting had caused him to flourish: the gospel had been so fully preached in that area that there was no more place in the region left where he needed to minister. (Romans 15:19, 23) Paul matched his gift – his unique ability to explain the gospel of salvation – to a worldwide audience. He explained to the church at Rome that he actually felt an obligation to serve both Jew and gentile. (Romans 1:14) His sense of mission was primarily to the Jews, for whom he said that he was even willing to be accursed if it would serve as a catalyst to bring them to the revelation of the gospel (Romans 9:3); however, he recognized that the gentiles – who actually became the most fertile ground of his ministry – were also an area in which he could serve with his gifting (Romans 1:16). In Paul's zealous quest for areas of service, God actually had to step in and stop him from going into Asia with his revelation and give him a vision of the most fertile area for the service of his gift. (Acts 16:6, 9) In his seemingly non-ending determination to find a field of service where his gift could be applied, the apostle desired to eventually reach Rome, the very heart and soul of the current society, and then proceed to Spain, the furthest boundary of the then-civilized world. (Romans 1:15, 15:24) All this was the visible demonstration of the invisible impartation.

Although his whole life is a testimony of this fact, I'd like to point out just a few examples that poignantly illustrate the fact that Paul was constantly ready – no matter what the circumstances were – to preach the gospel. The very next day after he was stoned and left for dead at Lystra, Paul traveled sixty miles – possibly on foot – to Derbe and then stood up to preach and teach. (Acts 14:19-21) Even his imprisonments didn't stop his outreach – with Onesimus as just one example of the fruit that he produced while in chains. (Philemon 10) Finally, as he languished on death row – not knowing whether the next steps he would hear coming down the corridor would be those of the executioner to take his life or those of the parole officer to give it back to him – Paul vacillated between his desire to go to heaven to eternal reward and his desire to go to the world to help them find that reward. His final conclusion was that – no matter how strong his desire to end all the troubles of this world might be – his readiness to help others out of this world's troubles was even stronger! (Philippians 1:20-26)

Not Ashamed

Paul's third declaration about his mission is found in the next verse, "I am not ashamed of the gospel of Christ: for it is the power of God unto salvation to every one that believeth; to the Jew first, and also to the Greek." (Romans 1:16) To Paul, there was nothing about the message of the gospel that he found embarrassing or uncomfortable. We often use the expression "lightning fast" to symbolically speak of things that happen very quickly, but in Paul's case there was nothing symbolic about it – his life took an instantaneous one-hundred-eighty-degree turn when the blinding light of Jesus struck him on the road to Damascus. With that split-second conversion from wanting to eradicate the very mention of the name of Jesus to calling on that name as his Lord, Paul had an absolutely unquestionable assurance that this gospel was the real thing. With that kind of unshakable experience, there was never any reason for him to doubt or compromise that it would be equally effective in anyone else's life. That is why he boldly shared his testimony when he was put on trial. (Acts 22:1-21, 26:1-23) Paul knew that the gospel had changed his life and had no doubt that it would change the lives of anyone who would believe it; therefore, it became a non-negotiable that he should present it on every occasion possible so as not to deprive others of the same life-changing power he had experienced. For others who have not had such a to-the-core-of-your-being encounter with the cross, there might be some intimidation or trepidation concerning the gospel – but not so with the man who has become a missionary by seeing the cross!

But what saith it? The word is nigh thee,

even in thy mouth, and in thy heart: that is, the word of faith, which we preach; That if thou shalt confess with thy mouth the Lord Jesus, and shalt believe in thine heart that God hath raised him from the dead, thou shalt be saved. For with the heart man believeth unto righteousness; and with the mouth confession is made unto salvation. For the scripture saith, Whosoever believeth on him shall not be ashamed. (Romans 10:8-11)

Being ashamed of the gospel not only hinders us from having maximum impact; it literally eliminates the possibility of having any form of impact at all. Before enrolling as a freshman at a secular university, my parents and I visited the local church so I could find a church family in the city. Fortunately, there was a gentleman in the church who was a research chemist – the exact profession I was pursuing at the time. The similarity in interest sparked an immediate connection, and he agreed to pick me up each Sunday morning for church. On the first Sunday, I dressed in my suit and tie and walked down to the parking lot to await his arrival. As I left the dorm, one of the other students asked me where I was going. My response was, "Out" – as if it was I could fool anyone while wearing a suit and tie at ten o'clock on a Sunday morning. After realizing how cowardly it was of me to be ashamed of the fact that I was going to church, I decided to invite the young man to join me the next Sunday. He accepted the invitation, and before long there were so many students joining us each Sunday that we had to recruit other church members to help with the carpool. Eventually, the church had to start a new Sunday school class just for the guys from the campus. Later, we started a fellowship on the campus itself which spread to twenty-two other college campuses and impacted hundreds of lives. When I enrolled in seminary, I discovered that there were twelve students from those groups on the secular colleges who were then studying at the seminary, preparing for full-time ministry – impact that resulted from one decision to not be ashamed of the gospel of Jesus Christ, the power of God unto salvation.

But It Doesn't Stop Here

> According as he hath chosen us in him before the foundation of the world, that we should be holy and without blame before him in love: Having predestinated us unto the adoption of children by Jesus Christ to himself, according to the good pleasure of his will, To the praise of the glory of his grace, wherein he hath made us accepted in the beloved. (Ephesians 1:4-6)

Yes, Paul was a man who was destined by God to become His apostle and servant. But, he emphatically proclaimed that the same provision has been made for every believer. God has been working a plan for all of our lives – even from before the foundation of the world. Certainly, Paul "blew it" on a number of occasions when he could have listened to his relatives, his teacher, or even the martyr; however, he did eventually surrender to his destiny when confronted by Jesus Himself. Maybe we have similarly focused our lives on our own goals and ambitions and have ignored the signposts that God has placed in our paths to direct us toward His course for our lives. But, just like Saul of Tarsus, there is still an opportunity for us to take that detour off our own road and change our course to the one that God has mapped out for us.

In Proverbs 29:18, Solomon wrote, "Where there is no vision, the people perish." Perhaps there are two different levels on which we can understand this little phrase. The most obvious one is that people who have no vision perish. This certainly was the case with Saul of Tarsus – until his vision on the road to Damascus, he was perishing. No matter how much he accomplished, his life was nothing more than dung (Philippians 3:8) until he had that divine encounter. The second level of understanding is that until those who are called according to the purposes of God get hold of the vision God has for their lives – or more accurately, are gotten hold of by that vision and calling – the people that they are to minister to will perish. This was definitely the case with Stephen and all the Christians that Saul of Tarsus imprisoned prior to his conversion and the multitude of Jews and gentiles who would never have heard the gospel had he never come to them after his conversion.

One dramatic story in modern history is that of my mentor, Dr. Lester Sumrall. As a teenage preacher during the Great Depression, he traveled through the southern states preaching in one-room schoolhouses – an attraction that usually drew out the entire local population since there was no other form of entertainment available to these rural farmers. During the song service, as he waited to step to the front of the crowd to share his message one evening, the young evangelist fell into a trance. He never found out what happened next because he was too embarrassed to ask anyone. All he knew was that he came to himself the following morning with his white suit stained mud red from rolling all night long on the dirt floor. Apparently the crowd had walked out and left him in his unconscious state – taking with them the kerosene lantern that one of the farmers had provided since there was no electricity in this backwoods community. But there was one thing that he did know – what had taken place inside himself; for that night, he saw the world perishing. In a vision, he saw a highway crowded with masses of people with all sorts of strange clothing – garments that he would later Irecognize from his travels around the world were Indian saris, Bhutanese ghoes, Native American buckskins, Burmese lungies, Arabian burqas, Ceylonese sarongs, African dashikis, and Japanese kimonos. As the multitude neared the end of the road, awful horror flashed across each face as each individual realized that he was about to plunge off of a huge precipice. No matter how hard they tried, they could not overcome the momentum of the throng behind them pushing them ever closer to their horrifying fate of being hurled over the cliff – and into a lake of literal fire. It was at that moment that the Lord spoke to the young evangelist, "It's your fault." Recoiling in disbelief, Sumrall retorted, "But how can their fate be my fault? I don't even know these people!" Using a phrase that the young preacher later discovered to be a verse from the thirty-third chapter of Ezekiel, the Lord answered that if Lester knew that there was impending danger and didn't warn everyone possible, he would be held accountable for their final destiny in hell. Awaking from this vision, Lester Sumrall's life was forever changed as he set out on a quest to ensure that a million souls would be rescued from the highway to hell and set on their upward journey on the highway of holiness.

With the illustration of the Saul's experience on the road to Damascus and the story of Lester Sumrall's encounter in that darkened Tennessee schoolhouse, perhaps it would seem that our future can only be defined by blinding lights, angelic interventions, or earthquakes and tsunamis – but, I'd like for us to remind ourselves of the stories of a few other great individuals who also had maximum impact even though they didn't have such earthshaking encounters to set them on their journeys of destiny. Daniel never described a special call into the ministry. He simply acted upon what he knew as right, and God placed him in the position of a prophet. (Daniel 1:1-2) Apparently, he had learned at his mother's knee what was right and wrong, and he simply followed through on his convictions when placed in situations where he had to make important decisions. Samuel's call was so gentle that he had to be told that it was God calling him. (I Samuel 3:1-21) David's call didn't even come to David himself. It actually came to the prophet-judge Samuel who then told David that

God had called him. (I Samuel 16:11-13) What can we learn from these examples? Simply that God doesn't have to shout if you're not far away. You can only whisper a secret when you are close to your partner's ear. You have to speak loudly if your partner is across the room. If he's across the street, you may have to yell. Perhaps the dramatic calls don't necessarily mean that those people will have more dramatic ministries than those with the gentle calls. Certainly, we cannot relegate Daniel, Samuel, or David to second-rate ministries just because they didn't have thunder and lightning when they were called. On the other hand, perhaps the gentle call is – in a way – a compliment in that it signifies that the person was close enough to the Lord that God didn't have to shout to get his attention. The Apostle Paul had what could be listed as the most dramatic call of all, yet he was also very busy trying to destroy the work of God. Because he was so far from God's will, it took a blinding light to get his attention. Dramatic or gentle, the results can be the same – a man or woman ready to do the work of God with maximum impact.

Lightning bolts or lightning bugs – it doesn't matter how dramatic our vision may be. The only thing that matters is that we – like Paul – determine to not be disobedient to it. (Acts 26:19) Once we make that determination, we can go back and implement some of the Apostle Paul's techniques and methodologies – and have the same maximum impact that he experienced!

Paul's Prison "P"s

One of Paul's impactful ministries occurred in the city of Philippi – the first city that he visited in Europe. His initial visit may have been as short as just a couple weeks in that the account in Acts chapter sixteen says that he was there over one sabbath (verse 13) and then continued for many days before being arrested and thrown into jail (verse 18). Later, Paul returned to the same region for three months, but it is unclear as to how much of this time was spent in the city of Philippi. (Acts 20:1-6) Therefore, it is possible that the ministry he established in Philippi could have been the result of just a few days of ministry or the result of three months of investment. Even if he did spend the whole of this second period ministering in Philippi, it is still an incredible accomplishment to birth a viable congregation in such a short time. Certainly, the quality of the testimony that he planted in the city during his arrest and imprisonment in the city left a lasting impression that produced maximum impact. The story of Paul's prison stay in the Philippian penitentiary is recorded in Acts chapter sixteen. Notice how each step is characterized with a word starting with "P."

Prison

> And when they had laid many stripes upon them, they cast them into prison, charging the jailor to keep them safely: Who, having received such a charge, thrust them into the inner prison, and made their feet fast in the stocks. (Verses 23-24)

Praise

> And at midnight Paul and Silas prayed, and sang praises unto God: and the prisoners heard them. (Verse 25)

Provision

And suddenly there was a great earthquake, so that the foundations of the prison were shaken: and immediately all the doors were opened, and every one's bands were loosed. (Verse 26)

Protection – Not only did God protect Paul and Silas, they protected the jailer.

And the keeper of the prison awaking out of his sleep, and seeing the prison doors open, he drew out his sword, and would have killed himself, supposing that the prisoners had been fled. But Paul cried with a loud voice, saying, Do thyself no harm: for we are all here. (Verses 27-28)

Penance

Then he called for a light, and sprang in, and came trembling, and fell down before Paul and Silas, And brought them out, and said, Sirs, what must I do to be saved? (Verses 29-30)

Promise

And they said, Believe on the Lord Jesus Christ, and thou shalt be saved, and thy house. (Verse 31)

Preaching

And they spake unto him the word of the Lord, and to all that were in his house. (Verse 32)

Purging – The jailer purged the wounds on Paul's and Silas' backs with water, and Paul purged the jailer's sins with baptism.

And he took them the same hour of the night, and washed their stripes; and was baptized, he and all his, straightway. (Verse 33)

Party

And when he had brought them into his house, he set meat before them, and rejoiced, believing in God with all his house. (Verse 34)

Proposition – The Roman officials made a proposition that would have avoided their having to face their error of unjustly arresting and beating Paul and Silas.

And when it was day, the magistrates sent the serjeants, saying, Let those men go. And the keeper of the prison told this saying to Paul, The magistrates have sent to let you go: now therefore depart, and go in peace. (Verses 35-36)

Privileges – Paul called upon his privilege as a Roman citizen and made the officials face their error.

But Paul said unto them, They have beaten us openly uncondemned, being Romans, and have cast us into prison; and now do they thrust us out privily? nay verily; but let them come themselves and fetch us out. And the serjeants told these words unto the magistrates: and they feared, when they heard that they were Romans. And they came and besought them, and brought them out, and desired them to depart out of the city. (Verses 37-39)

Parting

And they went out of the prison, and entered into the house of Lydia: and when they had seen the brethren, they comforted them, and departed. (Verse 40)

This story records how Paul's and Silas' praise and rejoicing precipitated in their deliverance and the salvation of the jailer and his whole family – not to mention the multiplication and growth that eventually produced a great parish in Philippi. As we read it, we should always remember that we all often find ourselves in one kind of a prison or another – physical, relational, emotional, physiological, or demonic. The same principles that worked for Paul and Silas will also not just open the prison's doors but literally destroy the prison from its very foundations.

The notable key that brought Paul and Silas out of that Philippian jail was their praise. Of course, we have no record of what their praises were, but knowing that the Jewish custom was to sing from the book of Psalms, I can't help but imagine that they must have voiced the words from some of the celebration songs of David's victories:

> The Lord is my rock, and my fortress, and my deliverer; my God, my strength, in whom I will trust; my buckler, and the horn of my salvation, and my high tower. (Psalm 18:2)
> He delivered me from my strong enemy, and from them which hated me: for they were too strong for me. (Psalm 18:17)
> He brought me forth also into a large place; he delivered me, because he delighted in me. (Psalm 18:19)
> Thou hast delivered me from the strivings of the people; and thou hast made me the head of the heathen: a people whom I have not known shall serve me. (Psalm 18:43)
> He delivereth me from mine enemies: yea, thou liftest me up above those that rise up against me: thou hast delivered me from the violent man. (Psalm 18:48)

Our fathers trusted in thee: they trusted, and thou didst deliver them. (Psalm 22:4)

They cried unto thee, and were delivered: they trusted in thee, and were not confounded. (Psalm 22:5)

He trusted on the Lord that he would deliver him: let him deliver him, seeing he delighted in him. (Psalm 22:8)

Thou art my hiding place; thou shalt preserve me from trouble; thou shalt compass me about with songs of deliverance. Selah. (Psalm 32:7)

The angel of the Lord encampeth round about them that fear him, and delivereth them. (Psalm 34:7)

The righteous cry, and the Lord heareth, and delivereth them out of all their troubles. (Psalm 34:17)

Many are the afflictions of the righteous: but the Lord delivereth him out of them all. (Psalm 34:19)

All my bones shall say, Lord, who is like unto thee, which deliverest the poor from him that is too strong for him, yea, the poor and the needy from him that spoileth him? (Psalm 35:10)

And the Lord shall help them, and deliver them: he shall deliver them from the wicked, and save them, because they trust in him. (Psalm 37:40)

But I am poor and needy; yet the Lord thinketh upon me: thou art my help and my deliverer; make no tarrying, O my God. (Psalm 40:17)

Blessed is he that considereth the poor: the Lord will deliver him in time of trouble. (Psalm 41:1)

The Lord will preserve him, and keep him alive; and he shall be blessed upon the earth: and thou wilt not deliver him unto the will of his enemies. (Psalm 41:2)

Thou art my King, O God: command deliverances for Jacob. (Psalm 44:4)

For he hath delivered me out of all trouble: and mine eye hath seen his desire upon mine enemies. (Psalm 54:7)

He hath delivered my soul in peace from the battle that was against me: for there were many with me. (Psalm 55:18)

For thou hast delivered my soul from death: wilt not thou deliver my feet from falling, that I may walk before God in the light of the living? (Psalm 56:13)

But I am poor and needy: make haste unto me, O God: thou art my help and my deliverer; O Lord, make no tarrying. (Psalm 70:5)

Thou calledst in trouble, and I delivered thee; I answered thee in the secret place of thunder: I proved thee at the waters of Meribah. Selah. (Psalm 81:7)

For great is thy mercy toward me: and thou hast delivered my soul from the lowest hell. (Psalm 80:13)

Surely he shall deliver thee from the snare of the fowler, and from the noisome pestilence. (Psalm 91:3)

Because he hath set his love upon me, therefore will I deliver him: I will set him on high, because he hath known my name. (Psalm 91:14)

He shall call upon me, and I will answer him: I will be with him in trouble; I will deliver him, and honour him. (Psalm 91:15)

Ye that love the Lord, hate evil: he preserveth the souls of his saints; he delivereth them out of the hand of the wicked. (Psalm 97:10)

Then they cried unto the Lord in their trouble, and he delivered them out of their distresses. (Psalm 107:6)

He sent his word, and healed them, and delivered them from their destructions. (Psalm 107:20)

For thou hast delivered my soul from death, mine eyes from tears, and my feet from falling. (Psalm 116:8)

My goodness, and my fortress; my high tower, and my deliverer; my shield, and he in whom I trust; who subdueth my people under me. (Psalm 144:2)

It is he that giveth salvation unto kings: who delivereth David his servant from the hurtful sword. (Psalm 144:10)

It was the congregation of believers that grew out of the seeds he planted in the city of Philippi that Paul admonished to continually rejoice to ensure their victory, "Finally, my brethren, rejoice in the Lord…Rejoice in the Lord always: and again I say, Rejoice." (Philippians 3:1, 4:4) In fact, he used the word "rejoice" ten times (verses 1:18, 2:16, 2:17, 2:18, 2:28, 3:1, 3:3, 4:4) and the word "joy" six times (verses 1:4, 1:25, 2:2, 2:17, 2:18, 4:1) in the short four-chapter book. To the Ephesians and the believers at Colossi, he defined his directive that such rejoicing should include the recitation of psalms, hymns, and spiritual songs. (Ephesians 5:19, Colossians 3:16)   Paul knew that thanksgiving and praise get our focus off ourselves and our problems; therefore, he commanded the Philippian believers that their lives be characterized by thankfulness, "Do all things without murmurings and disputings...Be careful for nothing; but in every thing by prayer and supplication with thanksgiving let your requests be made known unto God, " (Philippians 2:14, 4:6) Paul could write to the church about practicing praise and rejoicing in the midst of persecution because that is exactly the way he lived. Praise and worship were foundational to his ministry in the city of Philippi.   Not only was he beaten and imprisoned in Philippi, at the time of the writing of the letter, he was in prison and didn't know if he was going to be released or executed. When Paul wrote to the churches, he always stated that he was praying for them, but it was only to the Philippians that he said that his prayers were expressed with joy. (Philippians 1:6)

Praise and thanksgiving are dynamic keys to victory. We see an outstanding example of the power of thanksgiving in the story of Jesus and the ten lepers. Although all ten were healed, the Bible says that only one was made whole because he came back to give thanks. (Luke 17:11-19) The Bible says that the other nine were healed, but it gives us no indication that the parts of their bodies that had been eaten away by the leprosy were ever restored. If they had already lost earlobes to the leprosy, when they were healed, there was no more leprosy but the earlobes would still be missing. However, the one who came back and gave thanks was made whole. This means that he received a creative miracle in his body and his missing earlobes grew back. A dear friend of mine served as director of Nepal Leprosy Fellowship for more than fifty years. Among all the other things that I learned from this saint of God was one lesson that really made this story of the ten lepers come alive. She explained that the leprosy mission had two objectives – to heal the patients and to reconstruct their disfigured bodies. I obviously understood the significance of the first objective, but had never really considered the importance of the second thrust. Of course, I had been around enough lepers in my mission travels to know how unsettling it is to see these disfigured victims on the train or on the street. Even when the victim has been cured and is no longer contagious and is in no way a threat to society, the nubs he has for fingers, the missing earlobes, and the hole in the front of his face where a nose should be are enough to make everyone give him a wide perimeter. For these patients to be able to be accepted back into their homes and re-integrated into society, it is just as important that their deformities be dealt with as it is for their contagious conditions to be treated. Without reconstructive plastic surgery, these victims are doomed to the same miserable lives as outcasts that they had previously known. So it was with nine of the men who came to Jesus that day; they may have received certification from the priests that they were cured, but they would not be welcomed back by their wives, families, or employers. Only one – the thankful one who was made whole – was able to find welcoming arms waiting for him when he made his way back to his village. God will do so much for every Christian, but it seems that He does more for those who are thankful. When we get to the point of thanking God for what we do have rather than grumbling over what we do not have, we will find out how much more He is willing to bless us.

An equally powerful story of the authority of praise and worship is found in the familiar story of Jehoshaphat. (II Chronicles chapter twenty) The armies of the enemies were approaching, and Jehoshaphat's forces were far outnumbered; so the king declared a fast and sought the

Lord for His intervention. The Lord answered, "Ye shall not need to fight in this battle: set yourselves, stand ye still, and see the salvation of the LORD with you, O Judah and Jerusalem: fear not, nor be dismayed; to morrow go out against them: for the LORD will be with you." (verse 17) Then all the people of Israel worshipped the Lord. (verse 18)

God called them to the same revelation that He gave us in Ephesians chapter six concerning spiritual warfare. The verbs Paul uses are not verbs of struggle, but of standing in position with our authority, realizing that Christ has "spoiled principalities and powers, he made a shew of them openly" (Colossians 2:15) and now He is seated far above them (Ephesians 1:20-21) – and, best of all, we are accompanying Him in that position of dominion (Ephesians 2:6). God told Jehoshaphat to stand still because the battle was the Lord's; that is exactly what Paul was telling us in the book of Ephesians (verses 6:11, 6:14) – stand still and accept the victory that has already been won for us.

Worship is an important element in bringing us into victorious spiritual warfare. Jehoshaphat "appointed singers unto the LORD, and that should praise the beauty of holiness, as they went out before the army, and to say, Praise the LORD; for his mercy endureth for ever." (verse 21) Even though Jehoshaphat knew that praise and worship would be the important elements to win the victory, he did have his army dressed in battle array, ready for combat. Likewise, Paul tells us to "take on the whole armor of God." (verses 6:11, 6:13) We are not to act like there isn't a battle – we get dressed for the battle even though we know that God will do the fighting.

> And when they began to sing and to praise, the LORD set ambushments against the children of Ammon, Moab, and mount Seir, which were come against Judah; and they were smitten. For the children of Ammon

and Moab stood up against the inhabitants of mount Seir, utterly to slay and destroy them: and when they had made an end of the inhabitants of Seir, every one helped to destroy another. And when Judah came toward the watch tower in the wilderness, they looked unto the multitude, and, behold, they were dead bodies fallen to the earth, and none escaped. And when Jehoshaphat and his people came to take away the spoil of them, they found among them in abundance both riches with the dead bodies, and precious jewels, which they stripped off for themselves, more than they could carry away: and they were three days in gathering of the spoil, it was so much. And on the fourth day they assembled themselves in the valley of Berachah; for there they blessed the LORD: therefore the name of the same place was called, The valley of Berachah, unto this day. Then they returned, every man of Judah and Jerusalem, and Jehoshaphat in the forefront of them, to go again to Jerusalem with joy; for the LORD had made them to rejoice over their enemies. And they came to Jerusalem with psalteries and harps and trumpets unto the house of the LORD. (verses 22-28)

James told us to "count it all joy," not because we are to have the struggle but because we will come out from the struggle stronger than when we went in. (verses 1:2-4) When Jehoshaphat's army went out to fight the battle, they did not have the three days' worth of loot and booty in their hands that they eventually ended up with. They came into the battle with a genuine concern on their hearts. But they sought God until they finally came to the place that they could worship God, have faith in God, and draw nigh to God; then they used their praise to propel their spiritual weapons forward as they went into the battle. Instead of losing their houses, land, and families, they returned home with so much treasure that it took them three days to gather it all up. They came back better than when they went out to fight. James tells us that when we come to the temptation or trial, we must come to it with rejoicing because we know that on the other side we will be better off for having faced the conflict; Paul assures us that we will "not be ashamed." (Romans 5:1-5) Jehoshaphat's army came back full of rejoicing not only because their enemy had been defeated but also because they came back to Jerusalem with great wealth.

There is a victory that we will establish when we do warfare through praise. For Jehoshaphat there was a battle, there was a struggle, and there was warfare; however, he only had to stand and watch it happen! He simply observed the battle from his position of authority. Jehoshaphat came home that day as more than a conqueror. He did not have to fight the battle; he just reached out and took the reward from the battle.

Let me stress one important fact concerning Jehoshaphat's victory – it was manifested through praise, but the praise was established on the covenant relationship that Israel had with God. Notice that before Jehoshaphat commissioned the praisers, he reviewed and re-affirmed that covenant. It was only after he knew for certain God's promise and commitment to be Israel's defender that he was ready to rejoice. After purifying himself and his nation, Jehoshaphat was assured that they were in the right spiritual relationship to expect those covenant benefits. At that point, he was so full of faith that he called the army's accompanying band to begin to play the victor's march that they normally reserved for the march home after a victorious campaign. To Jehoshaphat, the victory had already been won so he didn't have to wait to see the final score; he could sing the triumphant song in advance! The power of his praise was based on the power of his faith in his covenant. So it is with us – we must be grounded in the foundational truths Paul is explaining if we are to see victory.

The power of a song or a jingle is tremendous. It has the ability to get into our subconscious mind and demand to be heard over and over and over. We use the term "earworm" to refer to these little songs that we just can't get out of our heads. I understand that Walt Disney's "It's a Small World" is considered to be the most difficult earworm to overcome. It is because of this kind of overwhelming force that jingles and songs can have that companies are willing to spend millions of dollars to get the right jingle to advertise their products. God wants to use exactly the same principle to get His victorious Word inside us through psalms, hymns, and spiritual songs. The scripture tells us to meditate on the Word – a term that means mutter it over and over and repeat it inside ourselves. (Psalm 1:2) The Holy Spirit tells us to sing and make melody in our hearts. Through that melody, the Word of God will get inside us to the point that we begin to bubble and churn with its truth. The words that go with that melody are being reinforced over and over, making us stronger warriors. This use of psalms, hymns, and spiritual songs is actually one way of redeeming the time. Even though we may not always be sitting down reading the Bible, the Word of God is bubbling on the inside of us because that melody keeps coming up.

One point to note about the prison incident with Paul and Silas is that the Bible specifically says that the other prisoners heard them as they praised. The lesson we can learn here is that we must not be bashful or afraid that we might not get our answer. Paul and Silas didn't cower in the corner and whisper their prayers and praises in fear of being embarrassed in case God didn't "show up." They boldly vocalized their worship, confident that God would not let them them down. You see, they understood the difference between their situation and their circumstances. We often use the words "circumstance" and "situation" interchangeably. We feel equally comfortable of speaking of our condition as being "under these circumstances" or as being "in this situation." However, these two words are not the same. In fact, they are radically different in their spiritual significance. "Circumstance" comes from two Latin words meaning the things that stand around us. "Situation," on the other hand, refers to where we are placed or where we sit. As Christians, we are seated with Christ in heavenly places far above all the principalities, powers, and wicked spiritual forces. We must never forget that we are situated in a superior position with every advantage over any difficulty that tries to defy us. If we fail to focus on this victorious truth, we may find ourselves believing that we are "under the circumstances." The first error with such a thought is that we have already abdicated our position of authority above the enemy by confessing that we are under the circumstances. The second error is that we have allowed our adversary to gain equal ground with us by allowing him to stand around us rather than be subjected under our feet. The last problem is that we have allowed him to get around or surround us. Since all our spiritual armor is described as frontal gear, we are equipped only for head-on confrontation with the enemy. The moment we give up that posture of direct confrontation and allow him to begin to surround us, we have exposed unprotected areas in our lives to him and have made ourselves vulnerable to his attacks. We must learn to aggressively maintain our situation and never fall under the circumstances.

It is interesting that in Paul's case, God sent an earthquake to get him out of the prison – unlike the angel that he sent to release Peter from his imprisonment in Acts chapter twelve. Now, don't get me wrong – I'm not belittling the miracle in Peter's life. I'd certainly not disqualify an angelic visitation and the supernatural loosing of the bonds and the miraculous opening of the iron gate – but I do see a significant difference between the two deliverances. Paul and Silas didn't just get out of jail – the structure was shaken to its foundations so that others were also released and no one could ever be held there again. Yes, Peter got out of jail, but the prison still existed – holding all the other prisoners and any future ones that would be assigned there. Paul's deliverance from the Philippian prison reminds me of the directive that God gave Jeremiah concerning his ministry – a commission to totally disrupt society as it currently existed.

Jeremiah lived in tumultuous times – times of the making and breaking of kings and kingdoms. He began his ministry during Josiah's sweeping reformation that turned the nation toward repentance from widespread idolatry; yet, Jeremiah continued to prophesy under the reigns of Jehoahaz, Jehoiakim, Jehoiachin, and Zedekiah who led the nation back into spiritual rebellion and pagan practices. Jeremiah was called to be God's spokesman during a period of storm and stress when the dooms of entire nations were being sealed. Not only did the smaller states of western Asia suffer as pawns in the power plays of such imperial giants as Egypt, Assyria, and Babylon but also these powerful empires were experiencing reorientation and restructuring so far-reaching that it was almost as if the nations had been tossed into a container, thoroughly shaken, and then spilled out again in a totally new array and order. Nothing was to look the same at the end of Jeremiah's ministry as it did before he began to prophesy.

History had brought the nations to the point that they were no longer able to get by with a "spank on the hand" – they were to be totally reshuffled and reinvented. During his watch, Jeremiah was to experience the kings of Israel being positioned and then removed from their position by the pharaohs of Egypt. He watched as the nation's rulers were taken captive and tortured by the Babylonian invaders. He witnessed the rape of Jerusalem and the razing of the temple. Additionally, he experienced the crumbling of the Assyrian Empire, the stripping of Egypt's power and glory, and the rise to power of the Babylonians. Amidst this chaos, turmoil, and upheaval among the nations, God demanded that the prophet speak destiny to the nations and their kings.

> See, I have this day set thee over the nations and over the kingdoms, to root out, and to pull down, and to destroy, and to throw down, to build, and to plant.
> (Jeremiah 1:10)

In our own personal lives, there come times when we need to go through this same kind of radical renovation where our old ideas and actions are not just altered – they need to be obliterated and replaced with new, living thoughts and deeds. "Therefore if any man be in Christ, he is a new creature: old things are passed away; behold, all things are become new." (II Corinthians 5:17) Let's look at each of the verbs in Jeremiah's mandate so that we can see how they can – and must – be applied to our own lives.

First, he was directed to "root out" – a term that signifies dealing with things at their very source. Unlike most of us, God is not satisfied with dealing with symptoms; He wants to get to the root cause of the problem. We humans can spend years of effort and millions of dollars trying to eradicate problems like human trafficking, drug smuggling, and arms dealing – but God knows that the problem doesn't lie in the illegal and inhumane activities. He

124

knows that the root is the greedy nature of man. "For the love of money is the root of all evil: which while some coveted after, they have erred from the faith, and pierced themselves through with many sorrows." (I Timothy 6:10) As long as men remain in love with money, every form of evil will continue to flourish in the world. It is only when Jesus is allowed into the hearts of the individuals who deal in human trade, drug marketing, and arms movements that the root cause will be eradicated and change will occur.

In II Samuel 12:1-6, we read how Nathan, the counselor to King David, craftily got to the root issue of evil in the leadership of the nation. He presented a hypothetical scenario for the king to judge. When David pronounced that the man who had stolen the supposed lamb should die for his crime, Nathan pointed to the king and announced that he was the sinner whose wrongdoing had inspired the story. David wanted to deal with symptoms, but the prophet bypassed the distractions to attack the evil root. When David composed Psalm chapter fifty-one as his repentance prayer for this crime, he acknowledged that his true sin was against God – not Bathsheba or Uriah. He realized that what happened in his physical life was only the fruit of the spiritual root of the problem – his loss of relationship with the Lord.

When God led the Israelites into the Promised Land, He directed that all the former inhabitants be totally eradicated to prevent them from becoming a "root that beareth gall and wormwood." (Deuteronomy 29:18) The people, in and of themselves, were not necessarily a problem. In fact, we see several occasions – most notably Rahab, who actually became part of the royal lineage – who were allowed to remain in the land as the Israelites took possession. However, the paganism that was so inbred into their mentality, lifestyle, and customs was detrimental to the people of God. The people themselves were only a symptom, but their idolatry was a root that had to be eliminated.

Job 5:3 speaks of foolishness as being a root. Hebrews 12:15 tells us that bitterness can also be a root. Certainly, we can deal with the actions that result from our foolishness or our bitterness, but if the root remains, we will only find more fruit popping up time and time again. That's the reason that Matthew 3:10 proclaims that the axe must be laid unto the root of the trees so that every tree that doesn't produce good fruit will be cut down and cast into the fire. The Lord isn't willing that we simply pluck off bad fruit; He wants the very root source of the corrupt fruit dealt with. Notice something significant in the story of the fig tree that Jesus cursed – the tree withered up from its roots. (Mark 11:20) The tree didn't simply wither – it withered from its very source. This was what the Apostle Jude would call "twice dead." (verse 12) From the same verse, we can understand that there is a level of death in which we stop producing fruit. This is the kind of death that Abraham and Sarah had experienced when they became too old to bear children. (Romans 4:19) They were very much alive; however, they were defined as dead because they could not produce offspring. Jude takes us a step further when he says that there is the possibility of being twice dead – not only unable to have fruit, but totally devoid of life. He describes this state as being plucked up by the roots. God wants that to be the case in our lives. He wants the roots of foolishness, bitterness, greed, and whatever else leads to bad fruit to be dealt with. He isn't interested in having us simply stop producing the fruit. He wants us to have the very potential of that error removed and destroyed.

The prophet's next directive is to pull down – a term that can be associated with the biblical teaching of pulling down strongholds.

> For though we walk in the flesh, we do not war after the flesh: (For the weapons of our warfare are not carnal, but mighty through God to the pulling down of strong holds;) Casting down imaginations, and every high thing that exalteth itself against the knowledge of God, and bringing into captivity every thought to the obedience of Christ. (II Corinthians 10:3-5)

For many years when I read this passage, I thought that the things that exalt themselves against the knowledge of God were ideas such as atheism that says there is no God or Hinduism that says that Vishnu, Krishna, Ganesh, or any one of the other millions of their deities is God, or Buddhism that claims Gautama to be divine, or even New Age that tells us that we all are gods. Then one day, the Holy Spirit prompted me to realize that even though I rejected all these pagan beliefs I still harbored thoughts that exalted themselves against God. When I questioned Him as to how it was possible that I could possibly have such thoughts, He probed me as to what I know about God. I responded that He is Jehovah Rapha, the God who heals all my diseases. The Holy Spirit then quickened to me the realization that any time I thought that my healing was in the medicine cabinet, a doctor's office, or a hospital that I was actually entertaining a thought that was exalting itself against what I really knew about God. He then asked me what else I knew about God. This time, I answered that I knew Him to be Jehovah Jireh, the God who provides all my needs according to His riches in glory. Again, He challenged me that every time I thought that my provision was in a bank loan, a higher credit card limit, working extra hours, or asking the boss for a raise that I was again entertaining thoughts that exalted themselves against the true knowledge of God. By the time that this little soul-searching session had taken me through several more truths about the Lord, I began to understand what this passage is really saying. It is a truth that can and must be applied to every area of our lives. Our weapons are strong enough to destroy the arguments against the knowledge of God. There are many areas of truth that we should know about God; however, for some reason, we don't comprehend and live in them. Why? Because there is an idea that has gotten into our heads that keeps the true knowledge of God from getting inside of us. We know that God exists, but we fail to attain a complete knowledge of who God is and what He does.

God is Jehovah Tsidkenu, which means that He is the God of our righteousness. The day that Jesus came into our lives, His righteousness came into us. However, the devil will come to each and every one of us with accusations to combat any awareness we have of this righteousness. If we open ourselves to these accusations, just like David's stone found that tiny eyehole in Goliath' armor, the devil will aim for this vulnerable spot. If that lie penetrates into our minds and we agree with it, the enemy begins to build a stronghold against the knowledge of God's righteousness within us. God is also Jehovah Rapha – the God who heals all of our diseases – but the devil wants to plant lies inside us saying that our ailment is either too big for God to heal or too insignificant for Him to notice. The truth is that God is just as willing to heal the little aches and pains as He is to heal major diseases. He is just as able to heal the most dreaded plague as He is to cure a minor ailment. We can go through all the redemptive names and qualities of God to learn what we should be thinking about God. Any time we allow thoughts contrary to these truths into our hearts, we have permitted the enemy to use his deceit to begin a stronghold in our minds.

Until David took the city of Jerusalem, it had never been captured. When Joshua came into the Promised Land, he defeated the king of Jerusalem, but the city itself was never taken. (Joshua 10:23-24, 15:63) The Jebusites boasted that Jerusalem was so secure that its guards were the blind and the lame men. (II Samuel 5:6) Its natural position made it virtually invincible; therefore, it was unnecessary to position the able-bodied soldiers there. These strong warriors were used elsewhere while the disabled veterans defended the city. In fact, the city actually defended itself since it was built on the top of high cliffs with deep ravines surrounding it. When an attack would come, all these handicapped soldiers had to do was simply to push boulders over the edge of the cliff upon the approaching forces – they did not need to be marksmen or skilled warriors. After David took the city, Jerusalem then became his stronghold. From the city of Jerusalem, we learn a lesson concerning strongholds: their power is in their natural position; we don't have to have a strong warrior inside a stronghold to be able to protect it because the stronghold itself is its own protection. The devil doesn't have to be strong. If he is able to fill our minds and hearts with lame ideas and blind assumptions, he can easily defend the strongholds of our lives.

Next God mandated Jeremiah to destroy – to totally eradicate – the undesirable qualities of the nations into which he was to prophesy. It is amazing that God never settles for mediocrity when He deals with sinfulness. He repeatedly used the term, "utterly destroy" in referring to the way His people are to deal with sin and sinfulness. (Leviticus 26:44; Numbers 21:2; Deuteronomy 7:2, 12:2, 20:17; Joshua 11:20; Judges 21:11; I Samuel 15:3, 15:9, 15:18; I Kings 9:21; II Chronicles 20:23; Isaiah 11:15; Jeremiah 12:17, 25:9, 50:21, 50:26, 51:3; Daniel 11:44; Amos 9:8). To utterly destroy something means to smash it into so many pieces that there is no possibility that it could ever be reassembled. It is His intent that all who are offensive to His rule are to be literally ground to powder. (Matthew 21:44, Luke 20:18) Once the root is pulled up, it must be crushed so that there is no possibility that there is enough life left in it to ever take root again. Jesus executed this kind of judgment against the devil in His resurrection, and He expects us to continue to demonstrate that same devastation against all the works of the enemy in our own lives.

> And having spoiled principalities and powers, he made a shew of them openly, triumphing over them in it. (Colossians 2:15)

> Now thanks be unto God, which always causeth us to triumph in Christ, and maketh manifest the savour of his knowledge by us in every place. (II Corinthians 2:14)

To throw down implies an even stronger and more forceful or deliberate act of aggression that pulling down. For instance, in Revelation 12:10 we hear the announcement of a loud voice saying in heaven, "Now is come salvation, and strength, and the kingdom of our God, and the power of his Christ: for the accuser of our brethren is cast down, which accused them before our God day and night." Satan has been kicked out of heaven since time immemorial and has been stripped of his power and authority since the crucifixion and resurrection of Christ; however, this prophetic moment speaks of a final dashing of Satan's personage in which all his activity will be brought to an end. The promise of the scripture is that all the evil influences of the devil and his demonic forces are to be thrown down to "ground zero" under the feet of Jesus. (I Corinthians 15:25-27, Ephesians 1:22, Hebrews 2:8) But more importantly, these diabolic forces are to be under <u>our</u> feet as well.

> Behold, I give unto you power to tread on serpents and scorpions, and over all the power of the enemy: and nothing shall by any means hurt you. (Luke 10:19)
> And the God of peace shall bruise Satan under your feet shortly. The grace of our Lord Jesus Christ be with you. Amen. (Romans 16:20)

Now we can see a fuller dimension of the statement in II Corinthians 10:5, "Casting down imaginations, and every high thing that exalteth itself against the knowledge of God, and bringing into captivity every thought to the obedience of Christ." We are not to simply arrest such thoughts, but we are to actually totally disable them and subjugate them under our authority, stomping them under our feet!

Next, Jeremiah is commanded to build up – a positive step after all the destructive actions he has been directed to take. This is a very important transition to go through if we expect to see true reformation. Simply destroying the evil in our lives or in the world we are called to minster to isn't sufficient. We must follow up with restoration. Jesus told us a story that powerfully illustrates this truth.

> When the unclean spirit is gone out of a man, he walketh through dry places, seeking rest, and findeth none. Then he saith, I will return into my house from whence I came out; and when he is come, he findeth it empty, swept, and garnished. Then goeth he, and taketh with himself seven other spirits more wicked than himself, and they enter in and dwell there: and the last state of that man is worse than

the first. Even so shall it be also unto this wicked generation. (Matthew 12:43-45)

When the evil spirit came back, he found the house clean. Apparently, this gentleman had done a good job of following all of Jeremiah's mandates so far. However, there wasn't anything in the house to fill the void that was left when all the evil had been rooted up, pulled down, destroyed, and thrown down. Since the man's house was vacant, the devil simply saw the "vacancy" sign as an invitation to take up residency again – only this time he brought in some companions to help him stake his claim even more definitively. In Luke 11:24-26, Jesus retold the parable and said that when the demon was cast out of the man, it found the man's house swept and garnished. When the demon returned, he brought seven more evil spirits with him. These new intruders were even more evil than the original one, and the end of that man was worse than before. Scripture says that the demon came back and found the man's house swept and garnished. Garnish actually has no functional value to a structure except that it makes it look pretty. Restaurants usually put some pretty little things on the plates to dress them up. The garnish may not be edible, and it may have no functional value to the meal prepared for us, but it is put on the plate just to make it look good. In this parable, the man kicked the devil out and he placed things in his life to make it look good, but they weren't of functional value. The man's problem was that he had nice religious decorations, but they had no function. Paul commands us not to do things for show as men pleasers or as eye service, but to do things out of a true heart that serves God (Colossians 3:22, Ephesians 6:6). First Samuel 16:7 says, "Man looketh on the outward appearance, but the LORD looketh on the heart." Man will look on the outside to see how garnished we are, but God looks on the inside and sees how we are functioning. First Corinthians demonstrates that even though we may have the outward garnish of the gifts of the Spirit, without the inward stability of the fruit of the Spirit, we are nothing, "Though I speak with the tongues of men and of angels, and have not charity, I am become as sounding brass, or a tinkling cymbal. And though I have the gift of prophecy, and understand all mysteries, and all knowledge; and though I have all faith, so that I could remove mountains, and have not charity, I am nothing. And though I bestow all my goods to feed the poor, and though I give my body to be burned, and have not charity, it profiteth me nothing." (I Corinthians 13:1-3)

Second Timothy 1:7 tells us, "For God hath not given us the spirit of fear; but of power, and of love, and of a sound mind." He takes away one thing – fear – and in its place, He gives us three things: power, love, and a sound mind. We often spend so much of our spiritual energy fighting the devil to get rid of one negative factor that we overlook our need to receive from God the fullness of His provision – provisions that bring us more and more into the full image of our Lord Jesus. God says that there are three things with which we must be filled: power, love, and a sound mind. When we are renewing ourselves in our mind with a sound mind, it has to be accompanied with power — Holy Ghost power. It has to be accompanied with love — God's nature in us. God has given us all three, not just one or two. Until we have all three of these divine characteristics operative in our lives, we will not reach our full measure of the stature of Christ.

The final stage of the reformation process is labeled as planting – causing something positive to grow in the place where the negative thing once flourished. Notice the words that the Lord later spoke to Jeremiah and their parallel in Isaiah, promising not to stop the process halfway through. God intends to see that whenever He removes a negative, there is a positive result that thrives in its place

Behold, the days come, saith the LORD, that I will sow the house of Israel and the house of Judah with the seed of man, and with the seed of beast. And it shall come to pass, that like as I have watched over them, to pluck up, and to break down, and to throw down, and to destroy, and to afflict; so will I watch over them, to build, and to plant, saith the LORD. (Jeremiah 31:27-28) And the LORD shall guide thee continually, and satisfy thy soul in drought, and make fat thy bones: and thou shalt be like a watered garden, and like a spring of water, whose waters fail not. And they that shall be of thee shall build the old waste places: thou shalt raise up the foundations of many generations; and thou shalt be called, The repairer of the breach, The restorer of paths to dwell in. (Isaiah 58:11-12)

In his letter to the Ephesians, Paul directed the believers that they not walk in the vanity of their minds as the gentiles do. (verse 4:17) Of course, it is easy to immediately define vanity as "emptiness" and go on – totally missing what this verse really has to say. To really catch on to what Paul was trying to communicate, we need to review the book of Ecclesiastes where Solomon defined exactly what vanity entails. In verse 1:14, he concluded that all the works or accomplishments that have been done under the sun are vanity. In verse 2:1, he summarized pleasure and entertainment as vanity. In verse 2:11, he concluded that all forms of employment are nothing more than vanity. Intelligence and education find their way to the vanity list in verse 2:15. Verse 2:17 embraced all of life as vanity. Being in a position of management or authority is also vanity according to verse 2:19. Being in a position to leave behind a legacy or inheritance is also vanity according to 2:21. Verse 2:23 adds diligence and a strong work ethic to the list. Living a moral life falls into the vanity category in verse 2:26. Being human as opposed to simply being a product of evolution still leaves us in the vanity category according to verse 3:19. Verse 4:4 tells us that "keeping up with the Jones" is also vanity. Struggling to make it "up the corporate ladder" falls in the vanity category in verse 4:7. Actually making it to that lonely place "at the top" is also vanity according to verse 4:8. Verse 4:16 describes even the "Rocky syndrome" of the underdog making unexpected achievements as vanity. Verse 5:10 pulls fiscal security into the discussion of vanity. Verse 6:2 amplifies this truth by adding that – even when it is obvious that wealth is a blessing from God – it can be fleeting and, therefore, vanity. Even long life and a prominent family do not ensure that one's life doesn't end as vanity according to verse 6:4. Verse 6:9 adds desire to the vanity list. Verse 7:6 adds a fool's comments. The inequities between good man and evil men fall on the vanity list in verse 7:15. Verse 8:10 tells us that the things that are forgotten as soon as our obituaries are written are nothing but vanity. The fact that just men seem to get the rewards of the unjust and vice versa is obviously vanity according to verse 8:14. Verse 9:9 says that even a happy home can belie the underlying vanity of the relationship. Verse 11:8 adds that even a long life can be only a camouflage for vanity under the surface. Youthfulness makes the list in verse 11:10. And the concluding summation is that everything is vanity is found in verse 12:8.

Well, that leaves us with essentially "no stone unturned." Business, industry, finance, education, politics, religion, entertainment, family – every area of human interest and endeavor is included as being vanity. Thus, it becomes obvious that the Apostle Paul wasn't saying that the gentiles don't have anything in their brains; rather, he was trying to tell us that the things that they occupy their minds with have no substance. Even if their plans and schemes move nations, transfer fortunes, and change the course of history, they are still vanity in God's sight. In that case, what is it that must be planted so that our minds as believers will not be focused on such vanity? Paul answered this question by sharing his own testimony in Philippians chapter three.

> Though I might also have confidence in the flesh. If any other man thinketh that he hath whereof he might trust in the flesh, I more: Circumcised the eighth day, of the stock of Israel, of the tribe of Benjamin, an Hebrew of the Hebrews; as touching the law, a Pharisee; Concerning zeal, persecuting the church; touching the righteousness which is in the law, blameless. But what things were gain to me, those I counted loss for Christ. Yea doubtless, and I count all things but loss for the excellency of the knowledge of Christ Jesus my Lord: for whom I have suffered the loss of all things, and do count them but dung, that I may win Christ. (verses 3:3-8)

In this passage, Paul gives us a pretty impressive list of accomplishments and pedigrees that would certainly qualify as the "stuff" of success in almost every dimension of life. Yet, he says that all these things are essentially dung vanity, if you prefer a little more polite description – to him. The one thing that he says is worthy of his consideration is "the excellency of the knowledge of Christ Jesus my Lord." The truth is that the New Testament abounds with confirmations of the fact that the knowledge of God is the essence of the Christian life. (Romans 1:28, 10:2, 11:33; I

Corinthians 15:34; II Corinthians 2:14, 4:6, 10:5; Ephesians 1:17, 3:4, 4:13; Colossians 1:10, 3:10; II Peter 1:2, 1:3, 1:8, 2:20, 3:18) It is the knowledge of our Lord and Savior Jesus Christ that must be planted in us to take the place of the vanity that will otherwise fill the thoughts of our minds and hearts. (Ephesians 3:17 Colossians 1:23, 2:7)

But does this mean that we must always go about thinking about God and Jesus like monks cloistered away from the rest of the world in a monastery somewhere? No – a thousand times no! Jesus prayed that we would be able to remain in the world while not being part of it. (John 17:15) We must find a place of balance where we can continue to live in and have an influence upon all the dimensions of society – yet not be sucked into the vacuum of their emptiness. The key is to realize that Christ is the true essence of every aspect of life – business, industry, finance, education, politics, religion, entertainment, family, and every other element of life. (I Corinthians 8:6, Ephesians 1:10, Colossians 3:11) The exquisite "Christ hymn" of Colossians 1:14-20 expresses this truth with such grandeur:

> In whom we have redemption through his blood, even the forgiveness of sins: Who is the image of the invisible God, the firstborn of every creature: For by him were all things created, that are in heaven, and that are in earth, visible and invisible, whether they be thrones, or dominions, or principalities, or powers: all things were created by him, and for him: And he is before all things, and by him all things consist. And he is the head of the body, the church: who is the beginning, the firstborn from the dead; that in all things he might have the preeminence. For it pleased the Father that in him should all fulness dwell; And, having made peace

through the blood of his cross, by him to reconcile all things unto himself; by him, I say, whether they be things in earth, or things in heaven.

In essence, the Jeremiah mission is not accomplished in our lives until we are able to look at every aspect of our lives and see Christ in it. Is there a dimension of Christ in each business deal that we arrange? Is there an aspect of Christ in every political move we make? Is the authority of Christ evident in our homes? Is Christ lord over how we spend our leisure time? Is Christ exalted in our religious activities? Is Christ the center of all we put our hands and hearts to? If not, then there is still something that needs the radical transformation of Jeremiah's ministry of rooting out, pulling down, destroying, throwing down, building, and planting.

Paul emphasized this same kind of all-out, jail-destroying, rooting-up, tearing-down action when he admonished the Galatian believers to move from simply living above fulfilling the lusts of the flesh to literally eradicating them, "This I say then, Walk in the Spirit, and ye shall not fulfil the lust of the flesh…And they that are Christ's have crucified the flesh with the affections and lusts." (Galatians 5:16-24) Don't just stop fulfilling the lusts of the flesh, mortify them! My wife serves as a chaplain in the local jail, and often speaks of the girls who are released only to wind up right back in jail within a few weeks – or, sometimes, days. You see, they are out of the physical jail but haven't torn down the emotional, psychological, financial, relational, and demonic prisons they are in; therefore, they wind up back in the physical jail as well.

The next significant move that we can identify in the story of the Philippian jail was that he saved the jailer's life. The Philippian jailer had beaten Paul and left him bound and bleeding while creepy, crawly things slithered across his back. Since his hands were tied, he could not defend himself from their invasion and infection. Yet, when the jailer was ready to commit suicide, Paul rushed to his rescue and saved his life – and then his soul. (Acts 16:22-34) I've often wondered if I would have responded so quickly when I saw the man who had treated me so cruelly ready to commit hari-kari. Perhaps, I would have let my emotional desire for revenge override my spiritual desire to obey Jesus' command, "Love your enemies, bless them that curse you, do good to them that hate you, and pray for them which despitefully use you, and persecute you." (Matthew 5:44) Probably only after it was too late, would I have thought to do the right thing. But Paul acted immediately to save the man – because Paul was not in the emotional prison of hate, resentment, or self-pity. He had torn those prisons down long before the physical jail came crumpling down.

In this story we find a few other principles that Paul applied resulting in maximum impact. One thing was that he seemed to recognize that people weren't his problem – otherwise, he would have taken revenge on the jailer. When people persecute or tempt us, we must remember that they are only instruments of the devil. In most cases, they really have no reason to try to hurt us, but they do so because they are captive to the forces that control them. In essence, we should think of abusers, pimps, drug dealers, and other people who damage our lives just like the person who passes a cold to us – they are sick, and can't help the fact that they are contagious. Directly related to this revelation was Paul's next principle – forgive. Paul took his relationship with the jailer one step further when he not only refused to hold resentment against him but also went so far as to forgive him and give him the greatest gift possible – leading him and his family to the Lord. Paul was able to have a powerful impact in the life of the jailer and in the city of Philippi as a whole because he was proactive – like

Jesus, he desired to minister rather than wanting to be ministered to.

One last point that I'd like to highlight in the story of Paul's experience in Philippi is that he demanded a public release. This may not seem significant at first; however, when we consider all the implications, we can see it was essentially his way of making a public testimony out of his test. It would have been one thing for the magistrates to privately acknowledge that Paul was right and they were wrong, but Paul insisted that it be made public to demonstrate the triumph of the gospel. In the book of Romans, Paul emphasized that our salvation is not actually complete until we make a public confession with our words (Romans 10:9-10) and a public demonstration through water baptism (Romans 6:4). After all, we were sick, depressed, addicted, and so on in public; so, we should go public with our deliverance. It is God's intent that we spoil the enemy by making a public show of him. (Colossians 2:15, II Corinthians 2:14, Revelation 12:11) When it looked as if the devil had won a victory over David by enticing him to commit adultery with Bathsheba and then to have her husband killed, the king won the victory of the guilt and condemnation by praying the dynamic prayer recorded in Psalm fifty-one; but note that the prayer ends with David's commitment to public worship – his way to testify openly and boldly that the enemy had been defeated in his life and that his sin had been reckoned with. Maximum impact comes when our deliverances and victories are demonstrated openly not only in the earthly realm, but also in the spiritual dimension. "To the intent that now unto the principalities and powers in heavenly places might be known by the church the manifold wisdom of God, According to the eternal purpose which he purposed in Christ Jesus our Lord." (Ephesians 3:10-11)

Surviving Shipwreck

One last concept that I'd like to explore before we leave the story of the Apostle Paul is the fact that he was a survivor. We have already seen in II Corinthians 11:23-28 that he lived through tremendous difficulties that could have crushed even the strongest of men – prisons, beatings, starvation, exposure to the elements, you name it. But he not only survived these circumstances – he thrived spiritually in them! In the story that we are about to study, you'll see that the apostle was able to "keep his head above water" when it looked impossible. But not only did he come through alive, he was able to rescue two hundred seventy-six others who would almost certainly have died had Paul not been there. And if that were not enough, he was able to instigate a revival on the island where he landed, bringing healing and salvation to many. Now, if that's not maximum impact – I don't know what is!

Yet, he realized that not all believers fared so well in trying times. When he told us in I Timothy 1:19 that some believers have made shipwreck of their spiritual lives, it seems to me that he was drawing upon his own personal experience of having survived three literal shipwrecks (II Corinthians 11:25) as a source for this nautical metaphor. Furthermore, it would seem to me that a shipwreck survivor might be able to give some worthwhile advice on how to come out alive on the other side of spiritual shipwreck. To begin our study, let's turn to Acts chapter twenty-seven that records what is possibly Paul's fourth shipwreck. As we read through the chapter, I'll stop just short of each point where a lesson is to be found, enumerate the principle, and then go on with the reading of the text to see how that truth is revealed in the saga.

And when it was determined that we should
sail into Italy, they delivered Paul and

certain other prisoners unto one named Julius, a centurion of Augustus' band. And entering into a ship of Adramyttium, we launched, meaning to sail by the coasts of Asia; one Aristarchus, a Macedonian of Thessalonica, being with us. And the next day we touched at Sidon. And Julius courteously entreated Paul, and gave him liberty to go unto his friends to refresh himself. And when we had launched from thence, we sailed under Cyprus, because the winds were contrary. And when we had sailed over the sea of Cilicia and Pamphylia, we came to Myra, a city of Lycia. And there the centurion found a ship of Alexandria sailing into Italy; and he put us therein. And when we had sailed slowly many days, and scarce were come over against Cnidus, the wind not suffering us, we sailed under Crete, over against Salmone; And, hardly passing it, came unto a place which is called The fair havens; nigh whereunto was the city of Lasea. (verses 1-8)

The first principle that we learn in this story of the ocean-going fiasco is to use some logic. If the captain would have only paid attention to what he already knew about the sea and the weather patterns, he could have avoided the entire incident. How often do we fall into the same trap of stupidity and pride of doing something against our own better judgment!

Now when much time was spent, and when sailing was now dangerous, because the fast was now already past, Paul admonished them. (verse 9)

142

The second principle is similar to the first, but on a spiritual rather than a natural plain, "Listen to your spirit." Many times there are occasions when that little voice inside tells us something that goes beyond what our brains are saying. Learn to recognize it as your spirit speaking under enlightenment of the Holy Spirit. I guess that I first learned this principle when checking out of a hotel in Texas. I had a long drive ahead of me and I wanted to keep my cash. In addition, I thought that since I had not used the credit card that month, I might as well pay the bill by check on the spot rather than to make a charge and have to write the check later to pay the credit card company. As I took out my checkbook, a little voice told me to use the credit card instead. Running through the reasoning I have just laid out, I ignored the voice and followed my brain. A few days later I regretted that moment of defiance when I had to pay a returned check fee that resulted from an error I had made in logging my checks and deposits. My brain had not caught my mistake, but my sprit knew that I was setting myself up for an overdraft. In all areas of life – as mundane as writing checks or as pivotal as making life-time decisions – we must learn to listen to our inner voice.

> And said unto them, Sirs, I perceive that this
> voyage will be with hurt and much damage,
> not only of the lading and ship, but also of
> our lives. (verse 10)

Principle number three might be, "Check out your motivation." In the case of Paul's shipwreck, the captain was motivated by money. A well-known little couplet says:

> Only one life will soon be past;
> Only what's done for God will last.

At every turning point and crossroads of life, it would be wise to recite that little rhyme before making a decision. If the choice is based on any motivation other than the cause of Christ, it should be reconsidered. It could be the difference between building with flammable wood, hay, and stubble as opposed to building with enduring gold, silver, and precious stones that will stand the test of time and the judgment of God. (I Corinthians 3:12)

> Nevertheless the centurion believed the master and the owner of the ship, more than those things which were spoken by Paul. And because the haven was not commodious to winter in, the more part advised to depart thence also, if by any means they might attain to Phenice, and there to winter; which is an haven of Crete, and lieth toward the south west and north west. (verses 11-12)

The next principle I see in this passage is to watch out for deceiving signs. Even when natural conditions indicate one thing, the truth is what God has said. I'm sure that we have all known since childhood that you can't judge a book by its cover, but do we live our lives in accordance to that understanding, or do we listen to temporal indicators rather than pressing in for eternal revelations about our situations? Do you remember the old commercial, "When E. F. Hutton speaks, people listen"? The unfortunate truth is that when God speaks, people don't listen. To avoid shipwreck of our faith, we must learn to believe God's Word over the report from the doctor, the newsman, and even the barber!

> And when the south wind blew softly, supposing that they had obtained their purpose, loosing thence, they sailed close by Crete. But not long after there arose against it a tempestuous wind, called Euroclydon. And when the ship was caught, and could not bear up into the wind, we let her drive. And running under a

> certain island which is called Clauda, we
> had much work to come by the boat: Which
> when they had taken up, they used helps,
> undergirding the ship; and, fearing lest they
> should fall into the quicksands, strake sail,
> and so were driven. (verses 13-17)

"Jettison the excess baggage" is principle number five. All of us carry around unnecessary – and deadly – emotional, material, and relational excess baggage that we must toss overboard in order to stay afloat in troubled waters. The only way to really get rid of those weights and be assured that they will not float back into our lives is to follow Peter's advise in I Peter 5:7 and cast our cares upon Jesus because He is the one who cares for us!

> And we being exceedingly tossed with a
> tempest, the next day they lightened the
> ship; And the third day we cast out with our
> own hands the tackling of the ship. (verses
> 18-19)

Probably the most important principle would be the admonition to not give up hope. One of Dr. Lester Sumrall's most memorable messages was his sermon I Did Not Quit in which he simply recited the opportunities that had been presented to him to just give up; but in every one of them, he determined to keep on going. I'll never forget his comparing himself to an old plow mule that just didn't know anything but to keep on trudging along. It was Winston Churchill who, with his jaw set in bulldog determination, demanded three times in a university baccalaureate address that the graduates, "Never give up!" Turning to the Bible, we find many illustrations including the shining example of Joseph in Egypt who didn't let a pit, Potiphar, or the prison make him give up on his dream of being the prince. Those who refuse to give up will never go down in the sinking ship!

> And when neither sun nor stars in many
> days appeared, and no small tempest lay
> on us, all hope that we should be saved was
> then taken away. But after long abstinence
> Paul stood forth in the midst of them, and
> said, Sirs, ye should have hearkened unto
> me, and not have loosed from Crete, and to
> have gained this harm and loss. (verses 20-
> 21)

It has been said that your attitude will determine your altitude; therefore, it is of utmost importance to apply the next principle of keeping a good attitude. Remember that you don't have to be under the circumstances just because you are in them.

> And now I exhort you to be of good cheer:
> for there shall be no loss of any man's life
> among you, but of the ship. (verse 22)

The next principle is number eight only in chronology, definitely not in rank of importance. "Wait for God to speak." Paul knew all along that everything was going to be all right, but he refrained from talking about it until he had heard directly from God about what to say.

> For there stood by me this night the angel
> of God, whose I am, and whom I serve.
> Saying, Fear not, Paul; thou must be
> brought before Caesar: and, lo, God hath
> given thee all them that sail with thee.
> Wherefore, sirs, be of good cheer: for I
> believe God, that it shall be even as it was
> told me. (verses 23-25)

Principle number nine would remind us that we must recognize that God's plan may not be as easy as our plan. In the great roll call of faith in Hebrews chapter eleven, we read about some of the heroes of faith who suffered greatly for their faith; yet, they were still listed as conquerors. I like to say that some were saved <u>from</u> tribulation, others were saved <u>in</u> tribulation, and still others were saved <u>by</u> tribulation – but they were all saved!

> Howbeit we must be cast upon a certain island. (verse 26)

At this point we must remember that just because God has spoken, the deliverance may not be immediate. We have already discussed Joseph's long wait for his promotion in Egypt, but we must realize that we, too, must wait in faith and patience for God's promises (Hebrews 6:12) and that, even though the vision God has given seems to tarry, it will come at the appointed time (Habakkuk 2:3).

> But when the fourteenth night was come, as we were driven up and down in Adria, about midnight the shipmen deemed that they drew near to some country; And sounded, and found it twenty fathoms: and when they had gone a little further, they sounded again, and found it fifteen fathoms. Then fearing lest we should have fallen upon rocks, they cast four anchors out of the stern, and wished for the day. (verses 27-29)

A major truth to realize when facing shipwreck is to "keep on keeping on." It is so easy to let go of our faith and try to take matters into our own hands, but we must remember the principle that Paul taught the Galatians, "Are ye so foolish? Having begun in the Spirit, are ye now made perfect by the flesh." (Galatians 3:3)

> And as the shipmen were about to flee out of the ship, when they had let down the boat into the sea, under colour as though they would have cast anchors out of the foreship, Paul said to the centurion and to

> the soldiers, Except these abide in the ship,
> ye cannot be saved. (verses 30-31)

Simply put, the next principle would be, "Let go of your own life support system." In other words, "Your way won't work, so try God's way!"

> Then the soldiers cut off the ropes of the
> boat, and let her fall off. (verse 32)

The next principle may seem a bit strange at first, "Don't get religious." Too often our religious ideas and actions actually bog us down when we need to be hearing a fresh word from God. That's why both Jesus and Paul warned us about the traditions of man. (Matthew 15:6, Colossians 2:8) We can see a good example of how religion can negate the realistic simplicity of a relationship with God in the story of King David's fast at the death of his illegitimately conceived son with Bathsheba. (II Samuel 12:15-23) Although he fasted while the boy lingered between life and death, he took food after the baby's death. His attendants thought that he should be more "religious" and continue the fasting and mourning after the boy's death, but David cut through the pretense of religion to explain the simplicity that his fasting during the baby's sickness had a purpose and that any further fast would be merely for appearance sake. In chapter fifty-eight of his oracles, the prophet Isaiah went to great detail to define genuine fasting as opposed to the ritualistic sham practiced by the religious leaders of his day. Unfortunately, his lesson was apparently not learned very well in that Jesus had to address the same issues again in the Sermon on the Mount. (Matthew 6:16-18)

> And while the day was coming on, Paul
> besought them all to take meat, saying,
> This day is the fourteenth day that ye have
> tarried and continued fasting, having taken
> nothing. Wherefore I pray you to take some

meat: for this is for your health: for there shall not an hair fall from the head of any of you. And when he had thus spoken, he took bread, and gave thanks to God in presence of them all: and when he had broken it, he began to eat. Then were they all of good cheer, and they also took some meat. And we were in all in the ship two hundred threescore and sixteen souls. And when they had eaten enough, they lightened the ship, and cast out the wheat into the sea. (verses 33-38)

The next principle we can learn in this lesson is that victory may not necessarily be paradise. Paul and his shipmates were rescued from the angry sea but found themselves on a hostile island in very uncomfortable conditions. Sometimes we need to learn to appreciate the deliverance we have received even though we still face further challenges.

And when it was day, they knew not the land: but they discovered a certain creek with a shore, into the which they were minded, if it were possible, to thrust in the ship. And when they had taken up the anchors, they committed themselves unto the sea, and loosed the rudder bands, and hoised up the mainsail to the wind, and made toward shore. And falling into a place where two seas met, they ran the ship aground; and the forepart stuck fast, and remained unmoveable, but the hinder part was broken with the violence of the waves. (verses 39-41)

The final principle may be a rather unusual one, but it warrants mention, "God will save the unworthy in the process of saving the righteous." God was so intent upon saving Paul that He gave him the lives of all two hundred seventy-six who were on the ship as a bonus. There are many such examples in the scriptures. In saving Noah, God also delivered his family, one of whom proved to be cursed. (Genesis 9:25) In saving Lot – whom Peter described as "just" (II Peter 2:7) – his two incestuous daughters (Genesis 19:31-36) were also delivered. When God was ready to totally destroy the children of Israel because of their rebellious nature, Moses stepped in between God and the people. In order to save the life of Moses, Jehovah granted mercy to the entire nation. (Exodus 32:32) For the sake of ten righteous people, God would have spared the cities of Sodom and Gomorrah. (Genesis 18:32) Jeremiah 5:1 declared that just one man who executed judgment would be enough to cause God to spare the city of Jerusalem from destruction. The New Testament teaches the principle that one righteous person in the home can sanctify the remaining unbelieving family members. (I Corinthians 7:14, I Peter 3:1) It also teaches that the church can provide a certain amount of spiritual covering over the ungodly within its influence; in addition, the church has the right – or should I say responsibility – to withdraw this umbrella of protection at times to let the wayward become aware of the consequences of their ways. (I Corinthians 5:1-5, I Timothy 1:19, Titus 1:20)

> And the soldiers' counsel was to kill the prisoners, lest any of them should swim out, and escape. But the centurion, willing to save Paul, kept them from their purpose, and commanded that they which could swim should cast themselves first into the sea, and get to land: And the rest, some on boards, and some on broken pieces of the

ship.   And so it came to pass, that they
escaped all safe to land. (verses 42-44)
With the Apostle Paul's example, we too can survive
– but not only survive, we can thrive. And not only that, we
can leave behind a maximum impact!

How Did Saul of Tarsus Become the Apostle Paul?

I will begin this chapter by begging your indulgence because I want to speculate on some concepts that are not specifically spelled out in the scriptures, but I believe that we can connect the dots without any real violation to reason or the sanctity of the text. We know that Saul was an excellent student of the Word of God in that he studied under the most notable rabbi of his day. (Acts 22:3) His experience on the Road to Damascus threw him into a total "tailspin" in that this encounter totally contradicted everything that he "knew" and believed. In his brain, Saul was totally convinced that Jesus was the greatest blasphemer, heretic, and charlatan that ever lived; however, his heart yelled out that Jesus was Lord even before he knew who it was that he had encountered in that blinding light. (Acts 9:5) We also know that once he was converted on the Road to Damascus and then baptized and filled with the Holy Spirit under the ministry of Ananias (Acts 9:17) he spent the following three years in Arabia without any further contact with Christians, especially those who could have taught him the truth of the gospel (Galatians 1:16-17). In essence, he went into the Arabian desert with his head spinning with questions and came back out of that desert with answers of such clarity that his explanation of the gospel has changed the world. This definitive revelation of the gospel was what transformed him from the rabbi of Tarsus to the preeminent apostle of the faith. Since we weren't in the Arabian desert with him, we can only speculate as to how he came by such revolutionary illuminations since his previous knowledge was totally based on the rabbinic interpretations of the Old Testament – ideas that he literally defined as dung. (Philippians 3:8) In II Corinthians 12:7-9, Paul speaks of the revelations that he had received and says that they were so abundant (in significance as well as in quantity) that the devil assigned a special messenger to torment him because of these insights – the fact that because of the abundance of his revelations, Satan sent a messenger to harass him in an attempt to keep the apostle from being exalted or recognized as an authority.   Obviously the enemy knew that such a clear presentation of the gospel would literally destroy any possible leverage he would have against the Christian faith. Elsewhere, he describes those revelations as mysteries that had been disclosed to him and even adds that these mysteries were truths that had been hidden throughout the ages – essentially waiting for him to unravel them: the mystery which was kept secret since the world began (Romans 16:25), the wisdom of God in a mystery, even the hidden wisdom, which God ordained before the world unto our glory (I Corinthians 2:7), and the mystery which hath been hid from ages (Colossians 1:26).

Perhaps – and this is the point where I stretch the line pretty far between the two dots – this revelation came to him through speaking in tongues and the accompanying gift of prophecy. Although there is no reference to when he began the practice of praying in tongues, we do know that the apostle was an avid tongues speaker. (I Corinthians 14:18) It is likely that he could have begun the practice of speaking in tongues as soon as he was filled with the Holy Spirit since this seems to be a biblical pattern – the believers in the Upper Room on the Day of Pentecost (Acts 2:4), Cornelius and his household (Acts 10:45-46), and the disciples in Ephesus (Acts 19:6). We can possibly add the believers in Samaria in that something occurred that was phenomenal enough to make Simeon the Magician want the ability to replicate it. (Acts 8:17-19)   We also assume that he was referring to himself when he wrote of a person who was caught up into paradise, and heard unspeakable words, which it is not lawful for a man to utter. (II Corinthians 12:4)

Notice the similarity of thought when he speaks of this experience being unutterable and the way he described speaking in tongues in Romans 8:26 as being in unutterable groanings. If all these dots do indeed connect, we can conclude that Paul spent much of the time that he was isolated in Arabia speaking in tongues so that he could get the revelation of the mysteries of God in his spirit, and then he pressed into prophecy so that the unspeakable truths in his heart became compensable to his mind in such a clear way that he could pen them to present a clear legacy of gospel truth for generations to come.

The reason I feel that Paul's avenue into these revelations was through speaking in tongues is his statement in I Corinthians 14:2, "For he that speaketh in an unknown tongue speaketh not unto men, but unto God: for no man understandeth him; howbeit in the spirit he speaketh mysteries." Some theologians feel that speaking in tongues is nothing more than some sort of emotional high that those who practice it use in order to escape reality. They say that the words themselves mean nothing and that the only value that the practice may bring is simply the euphoria that the speaker may experience for the few minutes that he or she is disconnected from the real world. On the contrary, speaking in tongues is not an escape from reality; rather, it is a divine connection to a level of reality that can only be approached through a supernatural connection.

The first thing that I'd like for us to notice in this verse is how Paul describes what happens when a person speaks in tongues – "in the spirit, he speaks mysteries." With this explanation, it might be easy to understand why some people would discredit the practice, saying that speaking mysteries, or unintelligible ideas, is pointless. But before we jump to any rash conclusions, it is important for us to remember that there is a radical difference between the two words "unintelligible" and "unintelligent." Just because something is inexpressible does not mean that it is senseless. In fact, the Bible gives us two powerful examples of things that are considered unspeakable, yet to be treasured – the joy of knowing Christ (I Peter 1:8) and the grace of God we experience in salvation through Christ (II Corinthians 9:14-15).

The second area that we should focus on in this verse is the fact that what is being spoken is defined as mysteries. Some might immediately respond that there is no point in focusing on things that are unsolvable – or, at least, unsolved. But exactly the opposite is actually true. To understand this point, let's take a look at some of the things that the Bible describes as mysteries:

>The kingdom of heaven or God (Matthew 13:11, Mark 4:11, Luke 8:10)
>
>Christ and God (I Corinthians 4:1; Colossians 2:2, 4:3)
>
>God's will (Ephesians 1:9)
>
>Christ and the church (Ephesians 5:32)
>
>The gospel (Ephesians 6:19)
>
>The faith in a pure conscience (I Timothy 3:9)
>
>Godliness (God was manifest in the flesh, justified in the Spirit, seen of angels, preached unto the Gentiles, believed on in the world, received up into glory) (I Timothy 3:16)
>
>Christ in you, the hope of glory (Colossians 1:27)

Certainly no one would dare to say that any of these subjects is unworthy of consideration and meditation! In that case, it does seem advantageous to speak of them in our prayers – even in prayers that are unintelligible to the natural mind.

The third area of focus that I would like to consider in this verse is that the tongues speaker is described as speaking to God rather than man. Now, let's apply a bit of basic logic to the matter at hand. Let's say that you were having trouble with your car, would you go ask the local grocer how to get it working properly? Obviously not – you'd go to the automobile mechanic. Why? Because he is the one who knows the answer to the mystery of why your car is not working properly. Need I really take the space on this page to draw out the analogy that it is the all-wise God to whom we need to address these mystery issues? Since it is obvious that we must have an understanding of God, Jesus, the gospel, God's will, His kingdom, and what exactly it means that Christ is in us, it is only logical that we need to address these issues to the proper authority and in the proper way. Romans 8:26-28 explains exactly how this happens.

> Likewise the Spirit also helpeth our infirmities: for we know not what we should pray for as we ought: but the Spirit itself maketh intercession for us with groanings which cannot be uttered. And he that searcheth the hearts knoweth what is the mind of the Spirit, because he maketh intercession for the saints according to the will of God. And we know that all things work together for good to them that love God, to them who are the called according to his purpose.

The Holy Spirit knows that we don't even know how to address the Lord properly concerning these mysteries; therefore, He assists us by praying with words that we would never be able to imagine, framing questions that we would not be able to construct. And He does this in tongues. Because He knows exactly what is in our hearts (our unintelligible – but not unintelligent – questions and concerns) and also knows the exact will of God (as opposed to our limited comprehension of it), He presents our requests in the exact manner that renders the wonderful

156

result of having everything work out just perfectly on our behalf! But as wonderful as that may be, it seems that there may be even more in this verse – the involvement of the very Son of God, Jesus Christ. Notice that the verse says that the one making intercession is the one who knows the mind of the Spirit – apparently someone other than the Holy Spirit Himself. Of course, we have to be cautious before we jump to conclusions because Greek at the time the Bible was penned didn't use capital letters. Therefore, the word "Spirit" could originally have been written with a small letter, indicating the human spirit rather than the Holy Spirit. In this case, the word "mind" would have to be understood not so much as the brain but the thinking process. If this is the case, then Paul is saying that the Holy Spirit knows what's going on in our spirits as we pray those unintelligible words, and He translates our requests to God in intelligible words. However, if we retain the capitalization, the verse is definitely speaking of someone other than the Holy Spirit since it is illogical to say that the Holy Spirit knows His own mind. In that we know that Jesus lives eternally to make intercession for us (Hebrews 7:25), the only reasonable option is that the verse is referring to Jesus. In this case, we have a multiplied benefit when we pray in tongues – not only does the Holy Spirit intercede on our behalf, but His concern catalytically generates more intercession from Jesus Himself – and we know that the Heavenly Father never denies the requests presented by His Son! (John 15:16, 16:23-27)

One other thing that we need to focus on is that Paul acknowledges that the mysteries that are spoken are from the spirit of the speaker – a concept that might be confusing to some readers because they automatically assume that the tongues come from the Holy Spirit. From the very first occurrence of this phenomenon, the scriptures made it plain that the believers in the Upper Room on the Day of

Pentecost did the speaking as the Holy Spirit gave them the words to say. (Acts 2:4) Thus, speaking in tongues is a joint operation of the inner heart of the believer and the Holy Spirit. As the spirit of the believer cries out for an answer from God, the Holy Spirit takes that request and molds it into the perfect prayer which is then verbalized in tongues by the outward physical being of the believer. As the mystery is unraveled, everything in the believer's life is supernaturally coordinated to work out just right.

Now that we have mentioned the physical and the spiritual dimensions of the believer, we need to also incorporate the soulical nature as well. And Paul does just that in I Corinthians 14:14, "For if I pray in an unknown tongue, my spirit prayeth, but my understanding is unfruitful." The believer's soul is still "out of the loop" at this point. That's why the prayers are considered mysteries – the mind doesn't figure out all the details. But the fact that the mind may still be at a loss doesn't make praying in tongues void or useless. If only we would think for a minute, we'd all realize that major aspects of our lives are controlled by things that don't register as logical in our minds. Let's take love for instance. Can any one of us give a logical, scientific, or mathematical formula or explanation for what happens when a mother sees her baby of the first time or the ongoing love between the parent and the child or what happens when that young man and young woman meet for the first time or how that infatuation turns to affection and matures into a life-long commitment? Of course not, but all of us have committed our lives to that thing called love, whatever it is. In the same way, we can pray mysteries in the spirit and still not have a logical intelligible resolution, but at the same time we will just know everything is all right. It all makes sense in our hearts even if our brains at still at a loss. Paul described this sort of relationship in Ephesians 3:19, "And to know the love of Christ, which passeth knowledge, that ye might be filled with all the fulness of God" – truths which he has referred to as mysteries in verses four and nine of this same chapter. How is it possible to know something that goes beyond knowledge? Obviously, he is expressing the event in which our spirits have experienced the content of the mystery while our brains are still trying to comprehend all the clues. This same message is echoed in I Corinthians 1:9-10, "But as it is written, Eye hath not seen, nor ear heard, neither have entered into the heart of man, the things which God hath prepared for them that love him. But God hath revealed them unto us by his Spirit: for the Spirit searcheth all things, yea, the deep things of God," in which he explains that there are truths and realities that are revealed in the spirit that are still not comprehended by the soulical personality.

Coupled with the gift of speaking in tongues is the gift of prophecy in which the mysteries that the spirit part of the believer has experienced become comprehensible to the intellect, "He that prophesies understands all mysteries." (I Corinthians 13:2) Since the Lord wants our total being to be blessed, He actually advocates that we desire this revelatory gift of prophecy above the other gifts which may only benefit one portion of our personality – for example healing that blesses the physical man or speaking in tongues that can bless the spiritual dimension while leaving the soulical unfulfilled. (I Corinthians 14:1) However, when prophecy comes forth, there is a total blessing that benefits us in every aspect. This is why the apostle stressed that the gathering of believers should focus on prophesy and revelation. (I Corinthians 14:6, 14:26)

Paul stressed that speaking in tongues should be primarily for one's personal use – likely for searching through the mysteries of God – while prophetic exposition of the mysteries of God should be the focal point of public ministry. In fact, he concluded that five words spoken intelligently are better than ten thousand words uttered in an unknown tongue. (I Corinthians 14:19) We can garner two significant thoughts from this summary statement. Considering that the average adult American male typically speaks ten thousand words per day, Paul's reference to this number of words in an unknown tongue emphasizes the point that quantity does not outweigh quality. But the real significance of this statement is found in his positive evaluation of the ability to communicate viable truth succinctly in just five words. In fact, this is exactly the quality that has made Paul the apostle whose writings have changed the world. All you need to do is visit a few Bible colleges and seminaries and take a tour through the libraries that a filled with shelf after shelf of books trying to explain Paul's thirteen short letters. Some of the greatest minds of the past two millennial have spent endless hours and filled uncountable books in their attempt to unpack all the godly mysteries that he exposed in his handful of writings – essentially five words in comparison to the volumes of revelation that have been deducted from them.

Let's take a quick look through some of Paul's statements to see if we can confirm the hypothesis that we have drawn so far. In I Corinthians 4:5, he wrote that we should never judge anything before the time – "until the Lord come, who both will bring to light the hidden things of darkness, and will make manifest the counsels of the hearts: and then shall every man have praise of God." Obviously, he is not referring to the Second Coming of Christ since that would leave every decision hanging until the end of time. Therefore, it is apparent that he is referencing the fact that the Lord can come in each present situation and make His will known. One likely example of this sort of divine intervention was in relationship to Paul's own ordination. In Acts 13:2, the Holy Spirit spoke and directed the elders in Antioch to anoint Paul and Barnabas for the mission work that they were to venture into. This directive came after these church leaders had spent some time in fasting and "ministering to the Lord." Is it possible that this ministry to the Lord was prayer in tongues? (I Corinthians 2:7, 14:2, 14:28) If so, this example can illustrate how we can invite the Lord to manifest Himself and give divine wisdom in matters that need supernatural direction.

The seventh chapter of I Corinthians reveals some interesting levels of confidence concerning the apostle's certainty in the advice that he is rendering in response to the questions that the church had raised concerning marriage. In verse six, he said, "I speak this by permission, and not of commandment." Apparently, he was convinced that his counsel was worthy of acceptance even though he couldn't attribute it one hundred percent to God as a verbatim directive. However, in verse ten, he wrote, "I command, yet not I, but the Lord." This time, he was unquestionable that the counsel he was giving was not his own thought, but the very edict of God. Contrast that with his evaluation of his advice in verse twelve, "But to the rest speak I, not the Lord." Here, the apostle readily admitted that this statement was his own and he was not going to "pull any punches" to try make it look as if he had a word from God on the matter. In verse twenty-five, he again confessed that his guidance was solely his own, "I have no commandment of the Lord: yet I give my judgment, as one that hath obtained mercy of the Lord to be faithful." Finally, in verse forty, he conceded that he was fairly confident that his counsel was in direct accordance with the mind of the Holy Spirit even though he wasn't certain, "I think also that I have the Spirit of God."

In comparison, Paul wrote with unequivocal assurance that he was hearing from the Holy Spirit in I Timothy 4:1, "Now the Spirit speaketh expressly." Even though this is the introductory statement to a new section in the epistle, if we view it as part of the entire letter we will recognize that it transitions from the concluding verse of the previous chapter in which Paul speaks of the mystery of godliness. In this perspective, we can see that the understanding of the mystery and the express message from the Holy Spirit can be seen as companion concepts. In such case, would it be too much of a leap of logic to assume that there could have been an element of revelation that came through Holy Spirit-directed prayer in tongues?

Paul made other references to the fact that the Holy Spirt bore witness to realities in his life. (Romans 1:9, 8:16) Additionally, he claimed that he received revelation directly from the Lord. (I Corinthians 11:23, Galatians 1:12) Perhaps this was his way of saying that his revelations were confirmed in the mouths of two or three witnesses (II Corinthians 13:1) – the Holy Spirit speaking the mind of the Father and the Son (John 16:13-16) Knowing how life-changing the revelations that he had received from the Holy Spirit were in his own life, Paul's most powerful prayer for the church was that they would also be transformed by this same divine revelation.

> [I] Cease not to give thanks for you, making mention of you in my prayers; That the God of our Lord Jesus Christ, the Father of glory, may give unto you the spirit of wisdom and revelation in the knowledge of him: The eyes of your understanding being enlightened; that ye may know what is the hope of his calling, and what the riches of the glory of his inheritance in the saints." (Ephesians 1:16-18)

But he doesn't stop with his own intercession, he directs us that we should also pursue the practice of Holy Spirit-empowered prayers, "And take...the sword of the Spirit, which is the word of God: Praying always with all prayer and supplication in the Spirit, and watching thereunto with all perseverance and supplication for all saints." (Ephesians 6:17-18) Notice the apparently intentional correlation with the Word of God and praying in the Spirit. It seems likely that Paul received his understanding of the Word of God – and the ability to actually pen words that would become recognized as the very Word of God – through praying in the Holy Spirit; therefore, he admonished the believers that he was discipling to pursue their spiritual connection with divine revelation through prayer in the Spirit. In I Corinthians 14:15, Paul made the determination that he would purposely pray in the Spirit as well as in the understanding. It is likely this is a reference to the practice of praying mysteries to God in tongues and prophesying the revelations back in an understandable language – the practice that changed him from Saul of Tarsus to Paul the apostle and the practice that can change us from average individuals to men and women who can make maximum impact.

Teach All Nations Mission

Teach All Nations Mission (TAN) is a global evangelical educational ministry birthed from the teaching ministries of Delron and Peggy Shirley. The name for Teach All Nations Mission was chosen to carefully indicate exactly what is the heart of the Shirleys' mission. TAN's commitment is to establish a solid foundation in national pastors and leaders so that they can help enrich their people. This vision is being accomplished by holding national leadership conferences and publishing and distributing Christian teaching materials in English and the local languages.

Someone accurately observed concerning the revival that is occurring in many parts of our world today that it is a mile wide but only an inch deep – the result of energetic evangelism by both missionaries and local Christians. Sadly, there is a marked shortage of teachers who are taking the next step in fulfilling our Lord's directive to teach them how to observe all that He has commanded. Therefore, Teach All Nations Mission has literally taken the words of Christ from Matthew 28:19, "Teach all nations," as its motto and mission statement.

TAN pays for the travel and lodging of handpicked leaders because Delron and Peggy want to invest into their lives but know that these third-world saints could never afford to come at their own expense. TAN always provides the meals for all the guests during these conferences. The ministry also furnishes solid Christian literature in their local language or in English for those who understand the language.

Delron and Peggy realize that the challenge is much bigger than what they can accomplish in person; therefore, they have determined to expand the scope of their vision. One area of expansion includes a scholarship fund that will allow selected individuals to obtain formal education in solid Christian colleges and Bible schools or through correspondence courses. The ministry has also assisted in building a Christian school in Zimbabwe and a Bible college in Nepal. Additionally, Teach All Nations assists the pastors and leaders they work with in times of need such as the tsunami in Sri Lanka, the hurricanes in Belize and the Turks and Caicos Islands, and the earthquake in Nepal.

Your gifts to and prayers for Teach All Nations will help the Shirleys continue their outreach to Christian leadership around the world.

Teach All Nations Mission
3210 Cathedral Spires
Colorado Springs, CO 8904
719-685-9999
www.teachallnationsmission.com
teachallnations@msn.com

Books by Delron Shirley

Bingo – A Fresh Look at Grace
Christmas Thoughts
Cornerstones of Faith
Daily Bible Study Series (Five-Volume Set)
Daily Ditties from Delron's Desk, Volume I
Daily Ditties from Delron's Desk, Volume II
Daily Ditties from Delron's Desk, Volume III
Daily Ditties from Delron's Desk, Volume IV
Daily Ditties from Delron's Desk, Volume V
The Great Commission – DOABLE
Dr. Livingstone, I Presume
Finally, My Brethren
In This Sign Conquer
Interface
Israel, Key to Human Destiny
Lessons from the Life of David
Lessons Along the Way
Living for the End Times
Maturing into the Full Stature of Jesus Christ
Maximum Impact
Of Kings and Prophets
Passion for the Harvest – A Missions Handbook
People Who Make a Difference
Positioned for Blessing and Power
Problem People of the Bible
Seeds and Harvest
So, You Wanna be a Preacher
The IN Factors
The Last Enemy
Tread Marks
Verse for the Day, Volume I
Verse for the Day, Volume II

You'll be Darned to Heck if You Don't Believe in Gosh
Your Home Can Survive in the 21ˢᵗ Century

By Peggy Shirley

Women for the Harvest

Available at:
teachallnationsmission.com